Praise for *Thomas Aquinas*

"Robert Barron has a genius for identifying and articulating the human sources for our intellectual inquiry, and here that of Thomas Aquinas, and how his rich talents were transformed by a vibrant life of faith. Anyone introduced to Thomas in a way that missed his mind and heart will find here a fresh appreciation of his teaching as well as his inner life."
—**David Burrell, CSC**, Theodore M. Hesburgh Professor Emeritus in Philosophy and
    Theology, University of Notre Dame

"Bishop Barron does a beautiful job of making the writings of Aquinas come alive for today."
—*The Catechist's Connection*

"Barron leads the reader beyond the technical theological language to the spiritual experience underpinning Thomas' writing."
—*Review for Religious*

"Spirituality with spine. . . . Barron's solid and accessible study is itself a fine example of what he admires in his master."
—**Michael Downey**, *America*

"A valuable and successful attempt to represent Aquinas in a refreshing and original manner as one of the Christian tradition's great spiritual masters."
—*Theological Studies*

Winner of the Catholic Book Award for Spirituality

THOMAS
AQUINAS

THOMAS AQUINAS

Spiritual Master

ROBERT BARRON

Published by Word on Fire Academic, an imprint of
Word on Fire, Park Ridge, IL 60068
© 2022 by Word on Fire Catholic Ministries
Printed in the United States of America

Cover design, typesetting, and interior art direction
by Cassie Bielak, Marlene Burrell, and Rozann Lee

Except where otherwise indicated, all translations of the works of Thomas Aquinas in this book
are from the Latin/English edition of the works of St. Thomas Aquinas published by the Aquinas
Institute in collaboration with Emmaus Academic in print and at https://aquinas.cc/.
Used by permission.

Excerpt from the English translation of the *Catechism of the Catholic Church* for use in the
United States of America copyright © 1994, United States Catholic Conference, Inc.—Libreria
Editrice Vaticana. Used by permission. English translation of the *Catechism of the Catholic
Church*: Modifications from the Editio Typica copyright © 1997, United States Conference of
Catholic Bishops—Libreria Editrice Vaticana.

Except where otherwise indicated, Scripture quotations are from the New Revised Standard
Version Bible: Catholic Edition (copyright © 1989, 1993), used by permission of the National
Council of the Churches of Christ in the United States of America. All rights reserved
worldwide.

First edition published 1996 by Crossroad Publishing Company

Second edition 2022

25 24 23 22   2 3 4

ISBN: 978-1-943243-79-2

Library of Congress Control Number: 2020925983

To Fr. Michel Corbin, SJ,
who first taught me to read Thomas Aquinas
as a spiritual master.

CONTENTS

CONTENTS

ACKNOWLEDGMENTS

There are many people whose influence and inspiration contributed to the writing of this book. I would mention first the Dominican Fathers of Fenwick High School in Oak Park, Illinois, who introduced me to the life and writings of Thomas Aquinas when I was a teenager. I would also acknowledge the impact of the numerous Thomists at whose feet I have studied over the years: Robert Sokolowski, John Wippel, and Thomas Prufer of the Catholic University of America in Washington, DC; David Burrell of the University of Notre Dame; Charles Meyer of Mundelein Seminary; and Michel Corbin of the Institut Catholique de Paris. Finally, I would like to thank two of my colleagues at Mundelein Seminary, Lawrence Hennessey and Raymond Webb, who in different ways pushed, pulled, and cajoled me into writing a better book.

INTRODUCTION

Thomas Aquinas' contribution to the Church and to Western culture in general has been so great that it is exceedingly difficult even to approach him, much less to understand him completely. He was a philosopher, scientist, mystic, theologian, scriptural commentator, and, in all things, a saint. For me, that last title is at the same time the most overlooked and the most illuminating. When one interprets Thomas merely as a rationalist philosopher or theologian, one misses the burning heart of everything he wrote. Aquinas was a saint deeply in love with Jesus Christ, and the image of Christ pervades the entire edifice that is his philosophical, theological, and scriptural work. Above all, Thomas Aquinas was a consummate spiritual master, holding up the icon of the Word made flesh and inviting others into its transformative power.

Toward the end of his life, after having struggled to compose a text on the Eucharist, Thomas, in an act of spiritual bravado not in keeping with his quiet nature, hurled his book at the foot of the crucifix, inviting Christ himself to pass judgment. According to the well-known account of this episode, a voice came from the statue of the crucified Jesus announcing that Thomas had written well concerning the sacrament and offering him a reward in recompense for his labors: "What would you have?" the voice asked. "*Non nisi te, Domine*" (nothing but you, Lord), responded the saint.[1] It is my conviction that this mystical conversation between servant and Master is a sort of interpretive key to the whole of Aquinas' life and thought: he wanted nothing more than Christ, nothing other than Christ, nothing less than Christ. He strove to walk in the path of discipleship and, in all of his writings, to show that path to others.

Now, I realize that my reader might, at this point, be wearing a puzzled frown. For many, Thomas Aquinas—whose writings are dry, recondite, often impenetrable—seems an unlikely candidate for the title of spiritual guide. His

---

1. Guillaume de Tocco, *Ystoria sancti Thome de Aquino de Guillaume de Tocco (1323)* 34.10, ed. Claire le Brun-Gouanvic (hereafter, *Ystoria*) (Toronto: Pontifical Institute of Mediaeval Studies, 1996), 162. See also G.K. Chesterton's discussion of the story in *Saint Thomas Aquinas: "The Dumb Ox"* (New York: Image Books, 1956), 109–111.

highly philosophical and abstract style appears to be diametrically opposed to the more earthy, affective, and personal approach of such recognized spiritual writers as, say, Meister Eckhart or John of the Cross. However, it is fascinating to note that both Eckhart and John of the Cross are profoundly marked by the theology of Aquinas. The former sat in Aquinas' chair of theology at the University of Paris and drank deeply from the wells of Thomas' wisdom. And John of the Cross' mystical poetry is built on the structure of Aquinas' theology.

One of the most significant blocks to appreciating Thomas as a spiritual master is simply the fact that we do not share some of his basic assumptions about the role and purpose of theology. Many commentators—including the Protestant Paul Tillich and the Catholic Hans Urs von Balthasar—have remarked that a great and problematic shift occurred around the year 1300.[2] At that time, theology came to be seen as a formal university discipline and was distinguished from what we might today call spirituality. The most prominent mystics, poets, and spiritual guides of the postmedieval period tended not to be theologians; rather, they stayed away from the centers of "scientific" thought, preferring, in some sense, to go underground.

But prior to 1300—that is, from the earliest centuries of the Church up until the time of Thomas Aquinas—there was no significant split between theology (talk about God) and spirituality. Many of the significant spiritual masters of the patristic period—Origen, Augustine, Pseudo-Dionysius, Ambrose—were what we would call theologians. All of these figures were interested, finally, in the transformation, conversion, and salvation of human beings. Their theology was not abstract speculation for its own sake; on the contrary, it was a sort of spiritual direction, an attempt to draw people into the imitation of Jesus Christ. It is interesting to note that neither Origen nor Augustine nor Jerome was writing for tenure or to impress an academic audience. Instead, they were writing, first and foremost, as pastors, passionately interested in the salvation of souls. Even the most challenging, philosophically oriented texts in the Fathers—and there are plenty of them—are meant not simply to illumine the mind but to open up the heart. It seems to me that if one had asked St. Augustine to distinguish between his theological writings and his spiritual writings, the saint would have been at a loss.

Though he differs with Augustine and the other Fathers on certain issues, Thomas Aquinas stands firmly in the patristic tradition that I have just described.

---

2. See Hans Urs von Balthasar, "Theologians and Saints," in *Explorations in Theology*, vol. 1, *The Word Made Flesh*, trans. A.V. Littledale with Alexander Dru (San Francisco: Ignatius Press, 1989), 181–210.

As he says in the very first article of the *Summa theologiae*, the entire purpose of theology is to raise believers outside of and beyond themselves to a union with the God who cannot fully be grasped. All that Thomas wrote is in service of the salvation offered in Jesus Christ. His thought is meant to be above all a guide, a series of landmarks on the journey into God.

Life and Writings

Thomas was born in either 1225 or 1226 in the family castle at Roccasecca near the town of Aquino, situated between Rome and Naples.[3] His father, Landulf, was a minor nobleman and his mother, Theodora, was descended from Norman and Neapolitan gentry. Thomas' family was deeply involved in the complex and shifting politics of the day that pitted pope against Holy Roman Emperor. In an attempt to improve the family's prospects and to mollify the Church, the five-year-old Thomas was sent to the Benedictine abbey of Monte Cassino to receive his basic education and eventually, it was hoped, to become abbot of that influential monastery.

Too many commentators have overlooked the importance of the young Aquinas' stay with the Benedictines. There he learned the rudiments of the contemplative life and there he fell in love with the Scriptures, especially the Psalms. The mature Thomas would understand theology as essentially an elaboration of the *sacra pagina*, the sacred page of the Bible, and he would present contemplation as the highest achievement of the human being. The seeds of these developments were planted, no doubt, at Monte Cassino. There is an illuminating story associated with Thomas' Monte Cassino period. It seems that at the age of five the future master of theology was attending a basic catechism class during which the teacher quite naturally was making frequent reference to God. With disarming honesty and straightforward curiosity, the youthful Aquinas rose to his feet and asked, "But, master, what is God?" It was a question he never ceased to pose throughout his life.

After nine years with the Benedictines, Thomas was compelled, for political reasons, to leave the monastery, and he took up what we would call undergraduate

---

3. For an acclaimed, scholarly biography that gives special attention to the spiritual dimensions of Saint Thomas' life and work, see the two-volume study of Jean-Pierre Torrell, *Saint Thomas Aquinas*, trans. Robert Royal, vol. 1, *The Person and His Work* and vol. 2, *Spiritual Master* (Washington, DC: The Catholic University of America Press, 1996–2003).

studies in philosophy at the University of Naples. There he studied under Peter of Ireland, a professor who dared to lecture on the metaphysical works of Aristotle, the Greek, pre-Christian philosopher whose thought had been condemned by several popes.

It is most important to pause here and to reflect on the revolutionary impact that Aristotle's thought was having on Christendom at this time. Certain works of the great philosopher—those dealing with logical and grammatical issues—had long been known and commented upon in Europe, but at the beginning of the thirteenth century, Aristotelian texts on metaphysics, the existence of God, and the nature of the soul began to arrive in the Christian world. These texts seemed to challenge many basic Christian beliefs concerning the immortality of the soul, creation, and the transcendence of God, and they were therefore formally suppressed by ecclesial authority. But to some Christian thinkers, these Aristotelian ideas were captivating, representing as they did a more rational, scientific perspective on the great questions of God and the world. Aristotle seemed to be urging Christians to turn to the concrete, to the real, to this world in order to appreciate the movement of God. To certain Christian philosophers, the thought of Aristotle was like a breath of mountain air blowing away the clouds of otherworldly mysticism and obscurantism that had for so long characterized theological speculation. In short, Aristotelianism was an exciting and dangerous revolutionary movement in the Christendom of the early thirteenth century, and young Thomas Aquinas became one of its most enthusiastic and important adepts.

The young radical became even more intensely countercultural when he embraced the other great revolution of his time: the mendicant movement. While still a university student at Naples, Thomas Aquinas took the habit of the preaching friars of St. Dominic. Like his contemporary, Francis of Assisi, Dominic de Guzman felt that the Christian Church needed to be revitalized through a return to the radicality and simple power of the Gospel message, and thus he gathered around him a band of brothers dedicated to lives of poverty, preaching, and unquestioning trust in God. Dominic sent his followers to the great urban centers, especially to university cities such as Paris and Bologna, where their preaching would have the profoundest impact. What was perhaps most impressive—and scandalous—about the Dominicans was that they were literally beggars, poor men going from door to door humbly but confidently asking for food and financial support. The presence of these mendicants, these fools for Christ, in the leading cities of Europe was, for some, a thrilling reminder that the Gospel lifestyle could still be concretely led; but for others, it was a shock and an embarrassment.

In becoming a Dominican, Thomas allowed himself to be swept up in the élan of this exciting movement, this back-to-basics evangelicalism. And therefore, as Josef Pieper points out, Thomas combined in his person the two great radicalities of his day: Aristotelianism and Gospel simplicity.[4] As an Aristotelian radical, he was opting for this world, for science, for reason, for the beauty of the senses, and as a Gospel radical, he was opting for the life of the spirit, for trust, for deep faith in the love of God. It was this splendid coming together of what were, for many, mutually exclusive commitments that animated and gave special color to all that Thomas would eventually write.

When Thomas joined this peculiar band in 1244, donning the costume of a beggar, he of course profoundly unnerved and disappointed his family. Keep in mind that they had hoped he would return to Monte Cassino, a well-appointed and richly endowed monastery, as a lordly abbot. Instead he had joined a strange and upstart group of radicals, throwing away as he did his wealth, his title, and his position. Chesterton avers that for a person of Aquinas' status to join the early Dominicans was comparable to running away and marrying a gypsy—or, in an even more contemporary comparison, to joining a cult.[5]

On his way to Paris to commence his formal Dominican studies, Thomas was kidnapped by his brothers and forced to return to the family castle at Roccasecca, where he was for all practical purposes kept as a prisoner in a tower. His parents and siblings hoped that eventually he would abandon his adolescent idealism and embrace a more respectable career choice, but Thomas stood firm, refusing various enticements and temptations that were placed before him. One famous legend has it that the young prisoner chased a prostitute from his cell, shouting and brandishing a torch—and no doubt frightening the girl half to death.[6] Another tradition has it that Thomas used his time in the tower to commit the entire Scripture to memory. Incredible as it sounds, such a feat is not entirely out of the question, given Thomas' prodigious mind. Indeed, according to some of his contemporaries, the thousands upon thousands of Scripture quotes in his theological writings were culled not from research but from memory, as if the saint were simply reading from a book.

In time, his family relented and the young friar was released and allowed to continue his Dominican studies. Recognizing his remarkable talent, Thomas'

---

4. Josef Pieper, *Guide to Thomas Aquinas*, trans. Richard and Clara Winston (New York: New American Library, 1964), 108.

5. Chesterton, *Saint Thomas Aquinas*, 39.

6. For a critical study that affirms the veracity of the prostitute narrative, see James A. Weisheipl, *Friar Thomas D'Aquino: His Life, Thought, and Works* (Garden City, NY: Doubleday, 1974), 30–33.

superiors sent the young man to the undisputed intellectual capital of Christendom: Paris. In the middle of the thirteenth century, the University of Paris was a magnet drawing scholars from all over Europe to hear and argue with the most subtle theological and philosophical minds of the time. The youthful and unruly students lived in crowded hostels on the left bank of the Seine and attended lectures, sometimes indoors, but also frequently on the streets, listening to various professors proclaiming their doctrines in the open air. The Paris style of theology—brash, skeptical, rational, somewhat irreverent—represented a departure from the dominant and more conservative monastic approach. In the schools of the Latin Quarter, it appeared as though any question, even the most daring, was fair game.

When he arrived in the new Athens of Paris in 1245, the young Thomas Aquinas found his context, his home. He also found his master and mentor in Albert, the Dominican scientist and philosopher, who, even in his own lifetime, was called "the great." Under Albert, Aquinas continued even more intensely the clandestine study of Aristotle that had begun with Peter of Ireland. In 1248, Thomas followed Albert to Cologne, becoming the great man's assistant and intellectual apprentice. While studying in Cologne, Thomas, taciturn, self-effacing, and by no means slender, was given the nickname "the dumb ox of Sicily." When Albert heard of this, he told his other students: "I assure you the bellowing of that ox will one day fill the world."[7]

In 1252, Thomas returned to Paris to begin what we would call postgraduate or doctoral studies in theology. For four years, he studied the Scripture and the standard theological textbook of the age, the so-called *Sentences* of Peter Lombard. These "sentences" were various patristic quotations that Lombard, a scholar-bishop of Paris, had gathered around central theological themes. Thomas' commentary on the *Sentences*—a sort of doctoral dissertation—announces early on the novelty and radicality of his approach. In 1256, when he was still only in his late twenties, Aquinas became a master of theology and began to lecture in Paris.

It is vitally important to pause here and consider what were the tasks and responsibilities of a master of theology in Thomas' time, for to understand the nature of this role is to grasp the heart of Aquinas' theological project. The first responsibility of a Parisian master of theology was, interestingly enough, to preach. The breaking open of the Word of God for the benefit of the students and faculty at the university was considered the paramount work of the professor. It is my contention that this preaching orientation can be seen in even the most

---

7. Guillaume de Tocco, *Ystoria* 13.60. See also Weisheipl, *Friar Thomas D'Aquino*, 26.

abstract and recondite of Thomas' writings. As a *magister* of theology, his purpose is never simply to satisfy the curiosity of the mind; rather, it is to change the lives of his readers, to transform their hearts, in a word, to move them to salvation.

The second task of the master was biblical commentary. Thomas' principal academic responsibility was not to lecture in philosophy or metaphysics or even systematic theology but rather to illumine and explain the *sacra pagina*, the sacred page of Scripture.[8] It is interesting—and highly regrettable—that among Aquinas' least known works are his biblical commentaries, precisely those presentations that were, at least in principle, at the very heart of his project.[9] Aquinas scholars are discovering only today the scriptural "feel" and focus in all of his more formally theological tracts.

The third and final responsibility of the *magister* was to raise and resolve those thorny questions that emerged from biblical commentary. The major forum for this theological exploration was the event that the medievals called a *quaestio disputata*, a disputed question. A disputed question took place in public, the master presiding over a large and sometimes raucous group of students and faculty. In a lively exchange, he would entertain objections from the floor, respond to the best of his ability, and finally resolve the question at hand, perhaps reveling in cheers or enduring catcalls from the floor. Thomas Aquinas was the most respected master of the *quaestio disputata* in Paris. Obviously, many professors carefully avoided this high-pressured and potentially embarrassing forum, but Thomas seemed to thrive in it, disputing far more often than any of his colleagues.

The best known of Aquinas' works—his great *Summa theologiae*, or summary of theology—is a reflection of this method. In the *Summa*, Thomas relentlessly raises question after question, stubbornly puts forward objection after objection, and finally gives his resolution and response. To some, this approach can seem tiresome and terribly dry, perhaps even a betrayal of the life-giving purpose of theology. But this is a misunderstanding, for behind the scholarly page, one must hear the fast-moving, engaging, perhaps irreverent and humorous give-and-take that inspired it—and above all the biblical and homiletic concerns that gave rise to it. Even in his most formal works, Thomas Aquinas is the spiritual master, hearing, responding to, and guiding the eager and curious students that surrounded him.

---

8. Jean-Pierre Torrell makes this point in *Saint Thomas Aquinas*, 2:vii.
9. Cf. Thomas Weinandy, Daniel Keating, and John Yocum, preface to *Aquinas on Scripture: An Introduction to His Biblical Commentaries* (New York: T&T Clark, 2005), esp. ix.

Thomas taught as a master in Paris between 1256 and 1259, and it was during this period that he began work on his *Summa contra Gentiles*, which some have considered to be a handbook for Christian missionaries working among the Muslims.[10] In 1259, Aquinas returned to his native Italy, and for ten years he served the papal court as a sort of official theologian at Anagni, Orvieto, Viterbo, and Rome. It was during these extraordinarily productive years that Thomas wrote many of his biblical commentaries, disputed questions, and massive commentaries on the works of Aristotle. And in the middle of the 1260s, Thomas began work on the masterpiece to which I have already alluded, the *Summa theologiae*.

In 1269, Aquinas returned for a second sojourn in Paris, staying in the City of Light until 1272. Then he journeyed once more across the length of Europe and established himself in his home province of Naples, where he continued work on the great *Summa* until shortly before his death in 1274.

Many have marveled at Aquinas' staggering output (his collected works fill nearly fifty folio volumes) in the course of a relatively short career.[11] Obviously, he was a great genius, but he was also a man who lived an intensely disciplined life. His day began with two Masses, one that he celebrated and a second at which he assisted, and continued, almost without interruption, as a cycle of reading, teaching, and writing. It is said that he dictated different works to as many as three secretaries at once, turning methodically from one to the other and rarely losing his train of thought. He would take a brief nap in the middle of the day, frequently dictating arguments in his sleep.[12] He was, I think it would be fair to say, a workaholic, rarely resting or turning away from the tasks at hand; absolutely on fire with the desire to know God, Thomas pushed himself relentlessly and probably dangerously.

There are many anecdotes centering around the theme of Aquinas' fits of abstraction.[13] Many of his contemporaries reported that Thomas was utterly unaware of what was placed before him at table, some even claiming that one of his brothers had to watch over the saint lest he put something inedible in his mouth. Another story has it that he was able to endure a dreadfully painful medicinal bleeding without complaint because he was so lost in contemplation.

---

10. For a fuller, critical discussion of this view of the purpose of the *Summa contra Gentiles*, see Brian Davies, *Thomas Aquinas's Summa Contra Gentiles: A Guide and Commentary* (Oxford: Oxford University Press, 2016), 9.

11. Torrell estimates that, on average, during his second appointment in Paris, St. Thomas composed nearly three and a half pages per day (*Saint Thomas Aquinas*, 1:240).

12. Guillaume de Tocco, *Ystoria* 18.85. See also Torrell, *Saint Thomas Aquinas*, 1:242.

13. See, for instance, Weisheipl, *Friar Thomas D'Aquino*, 235–236.

The best known vignette in this genre has to do with Thomas' somewhat comical dinner engagement with Louis IX, the saintly king of France. Against his will and at the urging of his superiors, Aquinas had accepted an invitation to dine with the king. In the midst of the lively and witty conversation, the philosopher sat in abstracted silence, as usual lost in thought. Then suddenly, much to the surprise and embarrassment of the other diners, Thomas brought down his fist upon the table, scattering plates and upsetting glasses. Thinking no doubt that he was still in his cell at the priory, Thomas said, "And that should settle the Manichees."[14] During the state dinner with the king of France, Aquinas had retreated into the recesses of his mind and had come up with an argument that could refute the dualistic heresy of the Manichees. One of Thomas' Dominican brothers reminded him rather sternly that his outburst constituted an insult to the king, but Louis himself, more concerned for truth than decorum, ordered that a scribe be sent to write down the friar's argument lest he forget it.

Thomas Aquinas was a mystic, someone whose life was literally ecstatic, caught up with God. Many of his brothers reported that, while saying Mass, Thomas would weep copiously, almost in a literal sense living through the Passion of Christ that he was celebrating and remembering. His *socius* and good friend Reginald of Piperno said that Thomas solved his intellectual problems not so much with thought as with prayer.[15] Wrestling with particularly thorny theological problems, Aquinas would rest his head against the tabernacle and, with tears, beg for inspiration. A careful and attentive reading of the texts reveals that this mystical passion, this ecstatic response to God, paradoxically suffuses all that Thomas wrote in his admittedly dry and laconic style.

No account of the life and spirituality of Aquinas would be complete without a reflection on the events immediately preceding and surrounding his death. In Naples, on the feast of St. Nicholas, December 6, 1273, Thomas was, according to his custom, celebrating Mass in the presence of his friend Reginald. Something extraordinary happened during that Mass, for afterward Thomas broke the routine that had been his for the previous twenty years. According to one source, he "hung up his instruments of writing," refusing to work, to dictate, to write. When his *socius* urged him to continue, Thomas replied very simply that

---

14. Guillaume de Tocco, *Ystoria* 43.15.

15. "Prayer and the help of God had been of greater service to him in the search for truth than his natural intelligence and habit of study." Bernard Gui, *The Life of Saint Thomas Aquinas* 15, in *The Life of Saint Thomas Aquinas: Biographical Documents*, ed. and trans. Kenelm Foster (London: Longmans & Green, 1959), 37. For a study of the place of prayer in the life and work of St. Thomas, see Paul Murray, *Aquinas at Prayer: The Bible, Mysticism, and Poetry* (London: Bloomsbury, 2013).

he could not. Afraid that his master had perhaps become mentally unbalanced, the younger man persisted until Thomas, with a mixture of impatience and resignation, finally replied, "Reginald, I cannot, because all that I have written seems like straw to me."[16]

To many, those are the most eloquent words that Thomas Aquinas ever uttered. After filling tens of thousands of pages with words about God, the great master very abruptly fell silent, convinced that everything he had written amounted to no more than refuse, perhaps persuaded that nothing finally can capture the strangeness and elusiveness of God. Some speculate that Thomas might have suffered a stroke (there is indeed some evidence that he was physically impaired after the December 6 incident) and others that he had what amounted to a psychological breakdown (many of his symptoms are consistent with burn-out, profound depression, or even midlife crisis).[17] Whatever explanation we offer, the simple fact of his remarkable silence remains.

In January of 1274, Thomas visited his sister but was scarcely able to speak to her. She described him as *stupefactus* (dazed or out of his senses). According to some sources it was during this visit that Thomas told Reginald that his work seemed like straw "compared to what had been revealed to him." If this is so, then Thomas' silence takes on a stranger and more mystical quality.

Summoned to the Second Council of Lyons in early 1274, the dutiful Aquinas set out for France but fell ill on the way. Anticipating his death, Thomas asked to be taken to the Cistercian monastery of Fossa Nuova. It was there that he died on March 7, some say after composing a commentary on the Song of Songs.

Thomas' Spiritual Path

It is intriguing to me how often Thomas uses the word "path" or "way" (*via*) in his writings. The whole of his master work, the *Summa theologiae*, is structured according to the way that leads from God to the world (*exitus*) and the way that leads from the world back to God (*reditus*). And the two paths come together precisely in the one who called himself the Way—namely, Jesus the Christ. It is only in recent Thomistic studies that the centrality of Christ has been adequately

---

16. Bartholomew of Capua, *From the First Canonisation Enquiry* 79, in *The Life of Saint Thomas Aquinas: Biographical Documents*, 109.

17. See, for example, Edmund Colledge, "The Legend of Thomas Aquinas," in *St. Thomas Aquinas 1274–1974*, vol. 1, Commemorative Studies (Toronto: Pontifical Institute of Mediaeval Studies, 1974), 26.

emphasized.[18] Jesus is not an afterthought for Thomas, but rather the cornerstone and summit of his whole theology.

All of Christian life begins with Jesus because in him we see the meeting of two ecstasies, that of God and that of the human being. For Thomas, the most impressive and powerful aspect of the Incarnation is its surprise. God's decision to join us human beings in our own flesh, in time and space, in all of the weakness and suffering of our finitude, is something in the presence of which astonishment is the only proper response. God must be a reality stranger, more powerful, more wonderful than we can imagine. Though God needs us not, though God is utterly self-sufficient, God nevertheless goes out of himself, in an unheard-of ecstasy, and becomes one of us. There is, in all of this, says Thomas, an *excessive*, ever-greater quality.

And the human being Jesus Christ, in perfect obedience and openness to this ecstatic God, forgets himself, goes out beyond himself in love, gives himself in a sort of imitation of divine ecstasy. And in this radical self-emptying, Jesus does not lose himself; rather, he becomes most fully himself, finding his deepest identity in union with God. This meeting of the ever greater, ever more surprising God and a self-transcending human being is the event of the Incarnation and the icon that presides over all of Thomas Aquinas' spirituality. Jesus Christ teaches us at the same time who God is (a power of love greater than we can imagine) and how we ought to respond to God (sheer obedience, sheer ecstasy, sheer wonder). Jesus expresses the inexhaustible mystery that is God and the never-ending adventure that is the journey into God.

From the standpoint of Jesus, then, Thomas presents his doctrine of God, or better, his anti-doctrine. Aquinas never tells us what God is, only what God is not. His entire approach is to undermine all of our idolatrous attempts to turn God into something understandable or controllable, something we could manipulate or avoid. No, he tells us in a variety of ways, the God who appears in Jesus Christ is a power that is consummately surprising, captivating, alluring. All of this strangeness is caught in Thomas' curious description of God as "simple."[19] As we shall see in a later chapter, this means that God is not a being like other beings in the world, that God is not even the highest or supreme being; God is rather Being itself, ungraspable, unknowable power. In describing God this

---

18. For just a couple of examples of this recent emphasis on the Christocentrism of Thomas Aquinas, see Fergus Kerr, "Christ in the *Summa Theologiae*," in *After Aquinas: Versions of Thomism* (Malden, MA: Blackwell, 2002), 162–180; Roger Nutt, "From Within the Mediation of Christ: The Place of Christ in the Christian Moral and Sacramental Life According to St. Thomas Aquinas," *Nova et Vetera* 5, no. 4 (Fall 2007): 817–841.

19. Thomas Aquinas, *Summa theologiae* 1.3.

way, of course, Aquinas is implicitly inviting his reader into a Christlike stance of obedience and wonder. Stop trying to reduce God to your level, he seems to say, and allow yourself to be drawn ecstatically into God's mystery. At the heart of Thomas' doctrine of God is, therefore, spiritual direction, the opening up of the heart.

It is from the same point of view that Thomas interprets the act of creation. Creation is not an act at the "beginning of time," not a once-and-for-all emanation from God; rather, it is an ongoing, continual gift that flows from the life and being of God. The world is totally dependent, from moment to moment, on the sheer generosity of the Creator. Aquinas calls this *creatio ex nihilo*, creation from nothing. When we recall the Christological roots of Thomas' theology, this teaching takes on great spiritual power. To be a creature means to be "nothing"—that is to say, pure openness and obedience in the presence of the Creator God. And, as the icon of Christ reveals, in this nothingness, in this ecstatic abandon, the creature most fully discovers herself. Various denials of the doctrine of creation *ex nihilo* are unmasked by Aquinas as sinful attempts to avoid obedience. To deny the Creator God is to live the illusion that one can find oneself apart from total surrender; it is to fly in the face of the Gospel injunction that those who cling to their life will lose it and those who lose their life for Christ's sake will find it. Hardly abstract, the teaching on creation seeks to place us, once more, in the stance and attitude of the incarnate Son.

When Thomas speaks explicitly of the human being, he is, once more, under the influence of the icon of Jesus Christ. The human being for Thomas Aquinas is an energy and a dynamism pushing out toward God, toward that infinite mystery revealed in the surprise of the Incarnation. The human person is an emptiness that will not be filled, a hunger that will not be satisfied, by anything less than God. He insists that we have all been made to lose ourselves, as Christ did, in obedient wonder. Any attempt to root our lives in something other than God— in ego, money, power, praise, pleasure—will set up an unbearable tension, a sort of crisis of the heart. To walk in the path of Christ is to walk according to that deepest destiny that God has placed within us. Furthermore, Thomas embraces the wonderful and mysterious doctrine of human "deification."[20] According to this teaching, the ultimate purpose or end of human life is a radical sharing in the very dynamism of God's own life. Aquinas is fond of quoting the patristic adage that God became human that humans might become God. For Thomas,

---

20. For a recent study that highlights the theme of deification in the *Summa theologiae*, see Daria Spezzano, *The Glory of God's Grace: Deification According to St. Thomas Aquinas* (Ave Maria, FL: Sapientia, 2015).

human life is not played out simply in the cramped quarters of time and space; rather, it opens up and out to the infinite being of God himself, to a participation in the perfectly responsive love of Christ.

There are many books written on the spirituality of Thomas Aquinas. Most of these concentrate on the subjects that have come to be recognized as spiritual as opposed to theological: prayer, contemplation, liturgy, etc. As I hinted above, it is my conviction that such an approach is anachronistic and antipathetic to the spirit of Aquinas. The spirituality of Thomas is found not only in those texts that we tend to recognize as spiritual but, perhaps most clearly and profoundly, in his doctrine of God, in his Christology, in his understanding of the human person, and in his lyrical theology of creation. These are not the academic dimensions of St. Thomas; rather, they are the places where the life-giving encounter between the divine and human is articulated. Aquinas is most remarkably a spiritual master precisely in those difficult but vibrant theological texts in which he wrestles with the God of Jesus Christ.

I have spent a good deal of time examining the texts of Thomas Aquinas in the course of my studies. I tended to approach this great thinker in a rational and critical way hoping to find illumination for my mind. But I discovered that under the influence of his writings my life began to change and more than my mind was illumined. I discovered, in short, what Thomas himself would have taken for granted: good theology is mystical, prayerful, and transformative, and its final purpose is to "know" God—that is to say, to be one with God in intimate communion. My hope is to share some of that life-changing wisdom in the course of this book.

Chapter One

JESUS CHRIST:
THE COMING TOGETHER
OF TWO ECSTASIES

I
t all begins, really, with a jest. The spirituality of Thomas Aquinas begins not with rational speculation, not with "proofs" and demonstrations, but with the wonderful, surprising, and wholly incongruous event of God becoming a creature. This jest is such that Christians have not ceased for the past two millennia to laugh at it in delight. In the light of this Incarnation, the strangeness and ungraspable mystery of God's love is, for the first time, *revealed* to human beings. The spiritual life, for Thomas, is nothing but the stunned and sustained reaction to this disclosure.

As was hinted at in the introduction, one of the most powerful spiritual critiques of Thomas Aquinas is that he thinks his way to God, basing his entire theology on rational proofs and philosophical arguments. There seems to be, some say, a sort of hubris or dangerous pride in this approach, a certain lack of docility and humility before the mystery of God. And from some Protestant critics one hears the charge that Thomas' thought is insufficiently Christological, that Jesus Christ is not the cornerstone and culmination of his system. If either or both of these charges were true, Thomas would be not only an inadequate theologian, but more importantly, a misleading Christian spiritual director.

What I hope to show in the course of this chapter is that neither reproach is justified. Aquinas never storms the gates of heaven with prideful reason, nor does he in any sense bracket or dismiss the unsurpassable event of God's self-disclosure that is the Incarnation. Rather, taking Jesus Christ as his point of departure, Thomas invites his reader into a stance of wonder and openness in the presence of the God whose generosity and love know no bounds. With the icon of the incarnate God in mind, Aquinas endeavors to lure us into an ecstatic appreciation of the ecstasy that is God, to find the God of self-forgetting love in our own self-forgetfulness.

I will explore these themes by looking at some of Thomas' texts dealing with, first, the event of revelation and then with the person and work of the ultimate "revealer," Jesus of Nazareth.

Revelation

The very first question posed in the *Summa theologiae* has to do with the nature of what Thomas calls *sacra doctrina*, or sacred doctrine.[1] What exactly is theology, this "talk about God," and why is it necessary? We recall that in the great universities of Thomas' time, philosophers were boldly using reason to probe the mysteries of nature and God. Aristotle's metaphysics, his study of the principles of being, seemed to allow the philosopher access even to the inner life and reality of God as cause and principle of the world. Given this rational confidence, why did the medieval scholar require the science of theology, or *sacra doctrina*?

Thomas' extremely illuminating answer to this question is the key to reading his entire project:

> It was necessary for man's *salvation* that there should be a teaching revealed by God beyond philosophical disciplines, which are investigated by human reason.
>
> Firstly, indeed, because the human being is directed to God, as to an end that surpasses the grasp of his reason.[2]

---

1. It is important to call attention here to the structure of the *Summa theologiae*. Thomas' great work is divided into three major sections, the *prima pars*, the *secunda pars*, and the *tertia pars*. The *prima pars* deals with God, Trinity, and creation; the *secunda pars* with the human being; and the *tertia pars* with Incarnation, Jesus Christ, and the sacraments. Each major section is subdivided into questions that are, in turn, subdivided into articles that specify the questions. An article begins with the statement of a question, e.g., Does God exist? The statement of the question is followed by the listing of several objections or counterpositions to the one that Thomas will take. After the objections, there is usually a *sed contra* (but on the other hand), a quotation from a philosopher or theologian or a scriptural citation meant to bolster and illumine Thomas' response. Following the *sed contra*, there is a *respondeo* (I respond), Thomas' formal answer to the question. Finally, Aquinas returns to the objections and, one by one, answers them, usually placing them in the context of the *respondeo*. A Thomist scholar might cite the *Summa* as follows: *Summa theologiae* I, q. 2, art. 3, ad. 3 (or 1.2.3 ad. 3 in the approach of this book), meaning, the first part of the *Summa*, question 2, article 3, response to the third objection. We recall from the introduction that this approach mirrors the style and practice of the "disputed question" in the medieval context.

2. Thomas Aquinas, *Summa theologiae* 1.1.1.

We require a science beyond the philosophical and natural sciences precisely because we human beings are oriented to an end that surpasses our powers of rational comprehension. We are destined to be united to a power that is beyond whatever the eye can see or the mind can know, beyond the world in all of its richness, beyond the web of contingent things. Here in some of the first lines of the *Summa* we see the theme of ecstasy and self-transcendence, a motif that will be repeated throughout Thomas' work: human beings are made to go beyond themselves, their end or purpose is to surrender themselves to a transcendent power.

And we notice something interesting in the subtle play of the language: there must be knowledge that goes beyond those sciences *built up by human reason—* that is to say, constructed by our minds and for our purposes. Purely "human" sciences are those that are expressions of the ego's desire to grasp and cling and control. Thomas seems to imply that even if these disciplines gave us some insight into God, they would not give us *saving* insight precisely because they are still too much in our hands, still too marked by the desire to *grasp* God, to have God, to know God in a manipulative way. But the God who is known in this manner is an idol, a creation of the ego—and thus a God who could in no way correspond to the deep and abiding desire for self-transcendence. It is not so much *what* the philosophical sciences tell us about God that is problematic; it is rather *how* they do so. Augustine said, "*Si comprehendis, non est Deus*" (If you understand, it is not God that you understand), and the Buddhists have a saying, "If you see the Buddha on the road, kill him."[3] Both of these maxims of the soul make a similar point: the moment *you* have the mystery or *you* see the divine, you have, in fact, ceased to have and failed to see. In insisting on God's *revelation* as the starting point of his project, Thomas is holding off the enormous tendency of the ego to control.

Sacra doctrina, or knowledge revealed by God, is necessary because the final goal of human life is not to grasp but to be grasped, not to rise up but to be raised up, not to ascend but to be drawn. The mind's hunger to control the world, to be the absolute power, must be disciplined before the human being can come to proper fulfillment. Of course, this theme of docility, passivity, and openness in the presence of the divine power is a commonplace among the great mystics. What I find intriguing is that Thomas Aquinas, the supposed rationalist, invokes

---

3. Augustine, *Sermones de scripturis* 117.3.5, in Patrologia cursus completus, series Latina (hereafter, PL), ed. J.-P. Migne (Paris, 1845), 38:664 (translation mine). For a contemporary English translation of this work see *The Works of Saint Augustine: A Translation for the 21st Century*, pt. 3: vol. 4, *Essential Sermons*, trans. Edmund Hill, ed. Boniface Ramsey (Hyde Park, NY: New City, 2007), 195–202.

it at the very beginning of his principal theological work. The spiritual master Aquinas is inviting the spirit to find itself in losing itself, to discover its richest power and destiny in surrendering to that reality that it cannot in principle control or have. In some ways, Thomas' entire understanding of God is implicit in this last statement. If the power to which human beings are oriented is radically and in principle ungraspable, uncontrollable, unreachable, then that power cannot be a thing or a being in or alongside the world. It cannot be one reality among many. It cannot even be the supreme or highest being. Rather, it must be a reality that breaks all bonds and that surpasses all the categories of thought. It must be that reality in whose presence awe and worship are the only proper responses. Whatever Thomas says about God throughout his writings flows from this great insight given in revelation.

The spiritual focus of this discussion becomes even sharper when we attend to the first words of Thomas' response: God's self-disclosure was necessary "for human salvation." God does not reveal himself in order to illumine our minds or satisfy our curiosity. Rather, God does so in order to move us, to shake us, to push us outside of and beyond ourselves in order that we might be *saved*. The implication is that without revelation we would tend to rest in ourselves, to remain comfortable with our ordinary lives among the finite things of the world. Revelation is a sort of spiritual wake-up, a radical reorientation of human beings, touching them at the center of their being and spurring them out and beyond. And thus *sacra doctrina*, theology, cannot be seen as a mere academic discipline; rather, as a codification of God's breakthrough, it is a matter of spiritual life and death, a way of conducting human beings to their final destiny.

And therefore what will follow in the rest of Thomas' great *Summa* is a type of spiritual direction, an articulation and explanation of that divine self-disclosure that is necessary for our salvation. It might be worthwhile to pause and reflect here on the fundamental meaning of the word "salvation," *salus* in Thomas' Latin. In common Latin parlance, *salus* meant "health," and thus an ancient Roman might have greeted his neighbor with the term "*salve*" (good health to you). It is only by analogy that *salus* came to mean "salvation" or "health of the soul." Interestingly, when the first Christians endeavored to designate the significance of Jesus Christ, they called him "healer": *sōtēr* in Greek, *salvator* (bearer of the *salus*) in Latin. In short, Jesus, precisely as the *revealer* of God, was experienced as the one who carries the healing salve, the soothing balm. As a Christian theologian, Thomas will explicate dogma and doctrine as expressions of the healing power of revelation, as signposts or landmarks on the journey into God, and therefore as solutions to the fundamental dilemmas and struggles of human life.

This existential quality of theology becomes even more apparent when Thomas moves to consider the seemingly dry question of whether *sacred doctrine* is a science. At first glance, it appears rather cold and abstract to refer to theology as a science: the self-disclosure of God reduced to principles and formulas. But Thomas' theological science, as he defines it, has nothing to do with disinterested knowledge at a distance. He tells us that *sacra doctrina* is a subalternate science—that is to say, one derived from the principles of a higher science. In a similar way, he explains, music is derived from, or subalternate to, the study of arithmetic. But what is the higher discipline from which theology draws its principles and perspectives? It is, states Thomas, the "science of God and of the blessed."[4] Now, the word *scientia* can designate an intellectual discipline, but it can also denote a direct, experiential type of knowing, a sort of knowledge through contact and touch. In what amounts to a delightful play on words, Thomas is telling us that the academic science of theology is drawn from the direct experience (*scientia* in the second sense) of God that is had by God himself and by the "blessed," those saints who are now enjoying the vision of God in heaven. He means that the science of sacred doctrine is a kind of participation in the inner life of God, or better, an anticipation of the beatific vision of God that is our proper goal as human beings. The ultimate source and orientation of theology is once again the transforming and transfiguring "taste" for God.

One of the problems involved with reading these texts of Aquinas on revelation is that we interpret them from a post-Cartesian, post-Enlightenment perspective. Descartes wanted a philosophy that was purely rational, constructed along the lines of mathematics and geometry, and the Enlightenment thinkers of the eighteenth century wanted all branches of human knowing to reflect the clarity and precision of Newtonian physics. In both perspectives, the ideal knowers are the detached observers, careful that their prejudices, desires, and traditions do not cloud the objectivity of their judgment. Thomas' science of God, his attempt to know the source and end of his life, has little to do with these more modern points of view. When Aquinas speaks of knowing God, his words have a biblical resonance and overtone. In a biblical perspective, "knowledge" can designate sexual union, the most intimate participation of one person in another: "How shall this be done, because I know not man?" (Luke 1:34 DRV) says the puzzled Mary to the angel of the Annunciation. In enticing us into knowledge of God, in drawing us onto the ground of *sacra doctrina*, Thomas Aquinas is offering us not clear and distinct ideas but rather a loving participation in God, a

---

4. *Summa theologiae* 1.1.2.

foretaste of heaven. He presumes that the one touched by this knowledge of God will be seared and shaped and overwhelmed by the contact.

Now, if it is indeed the case that Thomas Aquinas' theology is radically revelation based, why does it seem to depend so fully on rational arguments, on philosophy? Why does Thomas so often use language borrowed from natural science, from metaphysics, from pagan thought, sometimes, it seems, setting aside the terminology and style of the Scripture? In constructing his great Gothic cathedral of rational theology is he not indeed guilty of that charge of intellectual hubris that we alluded to above? Does he not, as Luther and some of the reformers implied, effectively deny the primacy of God's revealed Word in the Bible and in Jesus Christ, prostituting himself, as it were, with secularists and nonbelievers? In order to respond to these questions, and to grasp the master's spiritual strategy, it is vitally important to understand precisely how and why Thomas Aquinas uses philosophical tools in his work.

The wisdom of pagan philosophers and scientists, the insights of Jewish rabbis, the speculation of Muslim metaphysicians, all of it is employed by Thomas in his *pedagogical task* as teacher of revelation. Theology, he claims, in no sense depends upon this wisdom; it is not derived from it; it does not presuppose it or stand upon it. However, theology can use these intellectual treasures in order to entice and lure the human mind to a deeper vision of the truth of revelation.

Thomas tells us that theology must utilize philosophy, not because of some defect of its own, but rather because of the *debilitas* or weakness of the human mind.[5] Like many of the Fathers before him, Aquinas takes seriously the problem of the "fallen" mind. Like the will, the mind is profoundly and negatively affected by the power of sin. Instead of gazing naturally at the vision of God, the fallen mind tends to contemplate the things of the world, to concentrate upon the ordinary realm of creatures. In his *Commentary on the Gospel of John*, Thomas speaks of "inordinate lovers of the world" and those "who have fixed their eyes on the ground"—that is to say, whose minds are mired in the world of everyday experience.[6] This fallen mind is simply overwhelmed by the intensity of the light that comes from God's self-disclosure:

---

5. See *Summa theologiae* 1.1.5 ad. 2: "That [theology] thus uses [other sciences] is not due to its own defect or insufficiency, but to the defect of our intelligence, which is more easily led by what is known through natural reason (from which proceed the other sciences) to that which is above reason, such as are the teachings of [theology]."

6. Thomas Aquinas, *Commentary on the Gospel of John* 1.5.138, 1.4.121.

It may well happen that what is in itself the more certain may seem to us the less certain on account of the weakness of our intelligence, which is dazzled by the clearest objects of nature as the owl is dazzled by the light of the sun.[7]

The "weak" mind cannot easily take in the strangeness and otherness of God that appears in revelation; it is dazzled by such a vision. And thus it requires help in the form of a more natural, more down-to-earth wisdom. For Thomas, philosophical and scientific arguments are precisely these teaching devices, these tools, used to lead the fallen mind to a richer participation in the vision of God. In his language, they are handmaids of theology, servants of the divine science, "leading by the hand" (*manuducentes*) those who seek to see.[8]

In Thomas' own lifetime there were many voices raised in protest against his somewhat unconventional use of pagan and philosophical sources. His colleague St. Bonaventure charged that Aquinas was diluting the wine of the Gospel with the insipid water of pagan philosophy. But Thomas responded: "Those who use the works of the philosophers in sacred doctrine, by bringing them into the service of faith, do not mix water with wine, but rather change water into wine."[9] He was claiming, in other words, to ennoble and reanimate philosophy precisely by putting it into service of the divine science; he was allowing all provisional truth to find its proper place as a handmaid to the Truth itself.

This transformation of water into wine is an extremely instructive spiritual strategy. Thomas teaches us that all things, all objects, all stories, in some way can speak of the transcendent and infinite mystery that is given in revelation. He implies that the spiritual directors, the mystagogues, the theologians, should get up into any pulpit that they can, even those offered by "pagans" and "non-believers." Since *sacra doctrina* speaks not of some being sequestered above or alongside the world but rather of that all-embracing power that suffuses and sustains the universe, then all wisdom, even the most secularized, can be used to lead us to God. In a sense, Aquinas' method presupposes that a sharp distinction between the sacred and the secular, between nature and grace, is misleading, since all of nature is destined for the supernatural and can be used in its service. In the contemporary context, the follower of Thomas' spiritual strategy should feel at home utilizing the findings of depth psychology, sociology, anthropology,

---

7. *Summa theologiae* 1.1.5 ad. 1.

8. *Summa theologiae* 1.1.5 ad. 2.

9. Thomas Aquinas, *Commentary on the* De Trinitate *of Boethius* 2.3 ad. 5, trans. Armand Maurer, in *Faith, Reason, and Theology: Questions I–IV of His Commentary on the* De Trinitate *of Boethius* (Toronto: Pontifical Institute of Mediaeval Studies, 1987), 50. For more on Bonaventure's criticism of St. Thomas, see Weisheipl, *Friar Thomas D'Aquino*, 280.

and mythology. Thomistic spiritual guides do not establish *sacra doctrina* as an independent discipline, a sort of fortress careful to defend itself against the other sciences. Rather, inspired by the breadth of theology itself, they welcome the secular disciplines as allies in the spiritual quest.

The Event of Jesus Christ

Having examined some of the key texts at the very beginning of the *Summa*, we can say with confidence that Thomas Aquinas sees his entire theological and spiritual project as a response to the unexpected and overwhelming act of God's self-disclosure. Theology begins in wonder at the revealing power of God and ends in the rapture of the vision of God; the theologian, as spiritual master, explores the mystery in order to guide others to salvation. But what exactly is revelation and where does it come from? *How* is one grasped by the all-embracing power of being, lifted up beyond oneself and oriented to the pure communion with God? To answer these questions, we must turn to the third and final section of the *Summa*, more specifically to the questions and articles dealing with Jesus Christ. What becomes clear when we read the first questions of part one and part three together is that Christ himself *is* the locus, the event, of revelation, that energy by which the spirit is opened up and directed to God.

It is most instructive to attend carefully to the prologue to part three, Thomas' more poetic presentation of the scope and purpose of the last section of his masterpiece:

> Forasmuch as our Savior the Lord Jesus Christ, in order "to save his people from their sins" (Matt. 1:21) . . . showed unto us in his own person the way of truth, whereby we may attain to the bliss of eternal life by rising again, it is necessary, in order to complete the work of theology . . . [that] there should follow the consideration of the Savior of all and of the benefits bestowed by him on the human race.[10]

Here we see that Jesus Christ is the "way of truth," the path that leads us to that beatitude that is the ultimate goal of human life. Jesus is the *consummatio* of theology, the summing up, the *fulfillment*, the completion and goal of the spiritual project. Indeed, Thomas implies in this passage that Jesus' Resurrection from the dead is the signal that we are destined to rise again as well, that our final

---

10. *Summa theologiae* 3, prologue.

end is beyond the confines of this dimension. The conclusion is unavoidable: the illuminating revelation by which Thomas' theological endeavor begins and by which it is conditioned is Jesus of Nazareth, the definitive *via*, or way, to God. Jesus Christ is the light in which we see who God is (transcendent and alluring power) and who we are in relation to God (spirits oriented toward transcendence); he is the one in whom we appreciate the power that raises us up beyond ourselves to salvation. And therefore, far from holding a peripheral or incidental position in the Thomistic system, Jesus is the icon, the symbol that determines and shapes the whole of Thomas' theology and spiritual direction.

What and how Jesus reveals becomes clearer when we examine the articles dealing with the "fittingness" of the Incarnation. Aquinas argues that it was altogether fitting that God become incarnate precisely because in that surprising, unexpected act, the fullness and richness of the divine being could shine through:

> By the mystery of the Incarnation are made known at once the goodness, the wisdom, the justice, and the power or might of God—his goodness for he did not despise the weakness of his own handiwork; his justice, since on man's defeat, he caused the tyrant to be overcome by none other than man, and yet he did not snatch men forcibly from death; his wisdom, for he found a suitable discharge for a most heavy debt; his power or infinite might, for there is nothing greater than for God to become incarnate.[11]

It is the last comment that I find the most intriguing. Had God never become incarnate, human beings would never have developed an adequate sense of the greatness, the sheer transcendence, the unknowability of God. Prior to the Incarnation, Thomas implies, humans indeed worshiped and reverenced God, reflected on God philosophically, and honored God in various ways. But they always fell short of seeing the true extent of God, the strangeness and uncanniness of God's being. It is the condescension of the Incarnation, God's stooping low to join us as one of us, that "blows open" the mind, introducing the human spirit for the first time to an adequate conception of God's otherness and transcendence. What Thomas implies is this: only a reality *that is not a being in the world, even the supreme being*, could ever become a creature while at the same time remaining true to itself. The God who comes to join us in Jesus Christ must be a reality with a greater "stretch," a greater flexibility, a greater power of being than we could possibly have imagined. Whatever notion one might have had of God must be discarded in the presence of the Incarnate Word; even the highest titles of praise fall short of the glory revealed in the face of Christ. That

---

11. John Damascene, *De fide orthodoxa* 3.1. Quoted in *Summa theologiae* 3.1.1.

God creates and governs the world, that God loves and nurtures the beings of the universe, even that God guides us to a life after death—all of that was, to varying degrees, accepted and believed prior to the Incarnation. But that God would become a creature while still remaining God, that God would take on all of the "weakness of his handiwork," feeling limitation, suffering, death itself, that was simply unimaginable before Jesus Christ. That was simply too great to be hoped for, simply too ludicrous to be believed. In Paul's terms, it is "a stumbling block to Jews and foolishness to Gentiles" (1 Cor. 1:23). It is in this unheard-of surprise, Thomas hints, that true revelation takes place, for it is only in this shock that we realize how marvelous God is and therefore what a transcendent destiny is open for us.

This theme of the superabundance of God is further developed in a second argument. Thomas tells us that something is fitting or appropriate if it corresponds to nature. Thus, it is fitting that human beings engage in speech and thought because they are, by nature, rational animals. But the very nature of God is to be good, and, as Pseudo-Dionysius reminds us, it is in accord with the nature of the good to be "diffusive of itself," to express itself.[12] As we will see later in our treatment of creation, this effervescence of God can be seen in the exuberant multiplicity and variety of the universe, in the countless galaxies, in the dinosaurs, in the countless forms of life. God is undoubtedly playful in his self-expression. And therefore it is fitting that God, the highest good, should express himself in the fullest possible manner—and this, says Thomas, takes place only when God joins to himself a created nature, becoming one with creation. The key words in this argument are *maxime* (greatest) and *summo modo* (in the highest manner). Thomas is implying that it is only in the Incarnation that we can possibly know how good God is, since it is only there that the highest type of self-gift or self-expression takes place. In and through Jesus Christ, we can begin to glimpse for the first time the full range and intensity of the divine goodness, for only in Christ do we see the price that God was willing to pay, the self-emptying that God was willing to endure. This supreme and surpassing reality by which the human being is radically transformed and given a new ultimate purpose is none other than the strange God who is powerful enough to become powerless, great enough to become small.

I would like to return to that striking description offered by Pseudo-Dionysius, a theologian to whom Thomas is deeply indebted: the good is diffusive

---

12. See, for example, Pseudo-Dionysius, *The Divine Names* 4–5, in *Pseudo-Dionysius: The Complete Works*, trans. Colm Luibheid (New York: Paulist, 1987), 71–103. For the phrase "the good is diffusive of itself" (*bonum diffusivum sui*), see *Summa theologiae* 1.5.4 ad. 2, 1.27.5 obj. 2, 1–2.1.4, and elsewhere.

of itself. For the great mystic Pseudo-Dionysius, goodness is like a fountain, constantly overflowing, or like the sun, naturally radiating out, communicating almost in spite of itself. Or in more psychological terms, it is like a joyful person who simply cannot keep his good cheer to himself. The good spills over, speaks itself, shines forth. What the first Christians sensed in Jesus Christ is that God has utterly spoken himself, that God has indeed sent his Word, his very self, his own life. And, for Thomas Aquinas, it is precisely this insight into God's playfulness and capacity for self-offering that convinces Christians of the unspeakable *goodness* of the divine power. It is the self-forgetfulness of God, made visible in Jesus, that persuades us finally of God's superabundant generosity. If God had not become incarnate, if God had not joined us in our creatureliness, God would remain a limited, finite good, still to some degree restricted in love. In a word, the Christian discovers in Jesus Christ that God's being is *fully ecstatic*. God's nature is to go beyond himself, to step outside of himself, to forget himself in love.

This theme is further developed in the intriguing tension between the second objection and response. Animated by an artistic concern for harmony and balance, the objector maintains that it is particularly unfitting (*inconveniens*) for two things that stand at an infinite distance to be united.[13] Thus, goes the argument, it would be inappropriate for a painter to depict a human being with the head of a horse. But the divine and human natures are separated by an infinite distance, since the former is altogether simple and transcendent while the latter is finite and material. This counterargument is intriguing: there seems to be something inappropriate about the Incarnation. The combination of the divine and human appears to the aesthetically sensitive objector as a sort of monstrosity. Would it not be cleaner, he seems to imply, if the two natures simply remained distinct, each in its own proper sphere?

Once again, it is most important to attend to the subtle moves of Thomas' language as he responds to this objection:

> To be united to God in unity of person was not fitting to human flesh, according to its natural endowments, since it was above its dignity; nevertheless, it was fitting that God, by reason of his infinite goodness, should unite it to himself for human salvation.[14]

Aquinas holds that from the standpoint of the human being the coming together of the two natures would be *inconveniens*, inappropriate, since such a union

---

13. *Summa theologiae* 3.1.1 obj. 2.
14. *Summa theologiae* 3.1.1 ad. 2.

would be beyond the dignity of men and women. He seems to imply that there is nothing in the lowliness and sinfulness of human nature that would warrant the gift of the Incarnation, that would justify the condescension of God—and further that we human beings could never reach up to Incarnation on our own, forcing the issue as it were. That sort of sinful grasp would indeed be *inconveniens*, aesthetically displeasing, monstrous. However, when the Incarnation is seen from God's side, when it is appreciated as God's self-offering, as an expression of God's superabundant goodness, then it is entirely appropriate. When glimpsed from the standpoint of the ecstatic God, the Incarnation is, in its surprise, altogether reasonable. As we saw in the texts on revelation, Thomas battles here against the human pretension to rise up to God, to build a tower of Babel to heaven. The coming together of the divine and human is life-giving and salvific only when it takes place through the initiative of God; what saves us is *being lifted up* to a share in the divine life, not raising ourselves, but accepting God's self-offering as a gift, not as something due to us.

If article 1 is an exploration of the fittingness of the Incarnation from the side of God, article 2 is an analysis of the same issue from the side of the human being. Thomas wonders whether it was necessary for the restoration of the human race that God should become incarnate. We should note that Thomas is indirectly entering into dialogue here with his predecessor St. Anselm of Canterbury. In his book *Cur Deus Homo?* (*Why God Became Man*), Anselm had argued that the Incarnation was strictly necessary in order that the human race might be saved.[15] Anselm logically demonstrated that the Incarnation and cross were the necessary means to effect the forgiveness of sins and thus that God, in his goodness and justice, was practically obliged to enter into the human condition. Thomas distances himself from the position of Anselm, convinced that such a view puts too many constraints on the freedom and flexibility of God.

What one notices, in the course of the complex play of objection and response in this article, is once more the emphasis upon the divine surplus. The *Respondeo* begins with a distinction between two types of necessity: strict necessity and "convenient" necessity. Thomas says that food, for instance, is strictly necessary for the preservation of life, since that end could not be attained without food, whereas a horse is conveniently necessary for a journey in the sense that the journey is most pleasurably and economically undertaken on horseback.

---

15. See, for instance, Anselm, *Why God Became Man* 1.25, trans. Janet Fairweather, in *Anselm of Canterbury: The Major Works*, ed. Brian Davies and G.R. Evans (Oxford: Oxford University Press, 2008), 313: "it has been adequately demonstrated that, if we posit the non-existence of Christ, the salvation of mankind cannot be effected by any means."

In the first way, it was not necessary that God should become incarnate for the restoration of human nature. For God with his omnipotent power could have restored human nature in many other ways. But in the second way it was necessary that God should become incarnate for the restoration of human nature. Hence Augustine says (*De Trin.* 12.10): "We shall also show that other ways were not wanting to God, to whose power all things are equally subject; but that there was not a more fitting way of healing our misery."[16]

Though God could have brought human beings back into right relationship with him in a lesser way, there was no more fitting, no more extravagant, and no more perfect a way to inaugurate salvation than through Incarnation. God's becoming human was not a merely sufficient means to obtain the end of redemption; it was salvation through surplus and surprise. A gift is wonderful, but it is even more satisfying when it comes as a surprise. In one of his poems, John Shea paints the picture of a little girl who, upon hearing the Christmas story, turns over and buries her head under the cushion of the sofa: and this, says Shea, is the only proper response to the good news of the Incarnation.[17] Nothing could be more Thomist.

Following Augustine's lead, Aquinas spells out in detail the significance of this excess. Our faith is infinitely strengthened by contact with the sheer power of God's own mind; our hope is superabundantly enlivened by the conviction that God loves us so intensely that he gives us his only Son; our love is supremely awakened in response to God's overwhelming gesture of love; and, perhaps most importantly for the purposes of this book, our participation in the life of God, which is our proper end, is infinitely intensified through contact with the divinized humanity of Jesus Christ. Once more we notice the presence of superlatives: greatly, infinitely, supremely.

In short, it is none other than the excess of God's love expressed in Christ that shakes us out of our self-complacent finitude and orients us to the supernatural love that is our proper end; it is *in Christo* that we encounter the revealing God who is the ground and source of all authentic theological speculation.

We see the essentially Christological nature of revelation explicitly affirmed, once more, in Thomas' commentary on John's Gospel. In analyzing the grounds for the Incarnation, Thomas remarks that

creatures were not sufficient to lead to a knowledge of the Creator. . . . Thus it was necessary that the Creator himself come into the world in the flesh, and

---

16. *Summa theologiae* 3.1.2.
17. John Shea, "Sharon's Christmas Prayer," in *Seeing Haloes: Christmas Poems to Open the Heart* (Collegeville, MN: Liturgical, 2017), 36–38.

be known through himself. And this is what the Apostle says: "Since in the wisdom of God the world did not know God by its wisdom, it pleased God to save those who believe by the foolishness of our preaching" (1 Cor. 1:21).[18]

The Incarnation is the foolishness of God that shames the wisdom of the philosophers, the novelty that calls into question all that had been assumed to be the case concerning God. It is the surest sign that God is best described as ecstasy. Without the breakthrough of the divine power in Jesus, there could be no complete and saving knowledge of the Creator, that reality that is radically outside the net of contingent relations.

Commenting on the passage from the prologue of John's Gospel concerning the "seeing of the glory" of the incarnate Word, Thomas speaks of the healing power of God's presence in Christ:

Hence in order that the divine light might be seen by us, he healed our eyes, making an eye salve of his flesh, so that with the salve of his flesh the Word might heal our eyes, weakened by the concupiscence of the flesh.[19]

The fleshly humanity of Christ is the balm that heals the eyes of the soul, the light by which the hiddenness of God is revealed and hence the power by which the human being is raised up out of a preoccupation with finitude to a contemplation of her proper end. Once again, it is in this sense that Jesus is savior, the bearer of the salve that enables us to see.

After surveying these remarkable and often overlooked passages concerning the Incarnation, we can conclude that for Thomas Aquinas, Jesus Christ, God made human, is the light by which the goodness, the power, the strangeness, and especially the ecstasy of God are revealed. In his great leap out of himself, God discloses, superabundantly and overwhelmingly, who he is. In this ecstatic leap, God opens up the human mind and heart, illumines and heals the eyes of the human spirit, and thereby sets us on the path that leads to him.

Jesus as the Archetype of the Human Race

If Jesus Christ is the "place" and moment of God's revelation, then he must be, at the same time, the disclosure of the proper human stance with regard to God. We recall from the first question of the *Summa* that revelation is never abstract,

---

18. *Commentary on the Gospel of John* 1.5.141.
19. *Commentary on the Gospel of John* 1.8.182.

never received coldly or at a distance. On the contrary, it involves the lifting up and reorienting of the one who receives it. Thus, precisely as the bearer of divine revelation, precisely as the one who shows us the ecstasy of God, Jesus Christ also discloses what the human being should look like in the presence of God. And there is, in the thought of Thomas, a wonderful coming together of these two disclosures: Jesus reveals the ecstasy that is God in the measure that he, as a human being, is ecstasy before God. Jesus becomes transparent to God's self-forgetting because he, in his humanity, is nothing but self-forgetting love. In a word, the person of Jesus Christ is the joining of two ecstasies, the moment when the passionate human thirst for God meets the equally passionate divine thirst for us. Indeed, these two dimensions of revelation must be given together, since one implies the other. If human beings are not in a stance of obedience and love, we cannot see God, and if we do not see God, we cannot be in a stance of radical obedience. What appears in Jesus Christ, therefore, is a sort of interpersonal play of two freedoms, created and uncreated, each one in perfect openness and surrender to the other.

Before looking at some of the texts dealing with the humanity of Jesus, it is most important to recall that Thomas defends the classical Chalcedonian definition of the person of the Savior. He holds, in short, that in Christ there is a coming together of a divine and human nature in such a way that neither nature is compromised or overpowered by the other. The humanity of Christ is not a mere cover or veneer for his divinity, not, to use Karl Rahner's language, only a "livery" donned briefly by God.[20] Rather, it is an essential and fully integral aspect of who he is. Thus, for Thomas, it is altogether possible to speak of what pertains to Jesus precisely as a human being in relation to the revealing God, and in relation to us, his brothers and sisters.

It is to this issue that he turns in question 7 of the *tertia pars*, treating of the "grace of Christ as an individual human being." In article 1 of question 7, Thomas considers the following question: whether in the soul of Christ there was any habitual grace. Now, habitual grace is the ongoing, determinative, and transformative presence of God in the heart and mind of a human being. A real participation in the life of God, it is the power by which one is grafted on to the divine source. Aquinas insists that this type of grace is present in the soul of the Christ

> first, on account of the union of his soul with the Word of God. For the
> nearer any recipient is to an inflowing cause, the more does it partake of its

---

20. Karl Rahner, "Current Problems in Christology," trans. Cornelius Ernst, in *Theological Investigations* (Baltimore, MD: Helicon, 1961), 1:156n8.

influence. . . . Second, on account of the dignity of his soul, whose operations were to attain so closely to God by knowledge and love. . . . Third, on account of the relation of Christ to the human race. For Christ, as man, is the "Mediator of God and men," as is written in 1 Tim. 2:5, and hence it behooved him to have grace which would overflow upon others, according to John 1:16, "and of his fullness we have all received, and grace for grace."[21]

It behooves us to dwell on each of these three arguments that Thomas puts forward, for they reveal with great clarity Aquinas' view on the nature and importance of Jesus' humanity. First, the human heart of Christ is filled with habitual grace due to its proximity to the inflowing cause of grace that is the Word of God. The soul, the spiritual center of Jesus is, in other words, pressed close to the fountain that is God's ecstasy, God's tendency to flow out in love. The man Jesus is, if you will, a sheer receptivity to the outpouring of God's life, an ecstasy in the presence of divine ecstasy. Second, the soul of Christ is filled with grace because grace is necessary in order that any human nature can attain to God in knowledge and love. Once again we recall here Aquinas' understanding of the term *scientia* (knowledge) as intimate sharing in another. What Thomas tells us is that the humanity of Christ was raised up by the grace of God to a full participation in and experience of the divine reality. The presence of habitual grace in the soul of the savior means that Jesus is, in the depths of his being, a dialogue of love between the divine and the human, a play of invitation and response.

And then, in the third argument, Thomas arrives at the heart of the matter. There must have been habitual grace in the soul of Christ because Jesus stands as the *mediator Dei et hominum* (the mediator between God and human beings). As mediator, Jesus must have been in possession of a superabundance of grace so that this power might overflow from him upon the rest of the human race. There is a beautiful vision that stands behind Thomas' perhaps cold philosophical vocabulary: Christ is the human being who drinks deeply from the fountain of love that is God and who then overflows in love, pouring out what he has received on the rest of humanity. In his ecstatic embrace of God's ecstasy, Jesus becomes the condition for the possibility of our ecstasy before the divine source. Because he has been embraced, raised up, filled with love, we see the route that leads to life; because he was love before God, we see who we must become. A century before Thomas, St. Bernard of Clairvaux spoke of the kiss between the Father and Son, the mutual sharing of love between the two divine persons. And

---

21. *Summa theologiae* 3.7.1.

then, borrowing from the opening lines of the Song of Songs, he said that the Christian longs to be "kissed with the kiss" of Jesus' mouth, to receive, in other words, a share in what the Father has given to the Son.[22]

This theme of Christ as the mediator for all is a commonplace in the biblical and patristic tradition but is, unfortunately, too often overlooked in ordinary Christian piety and reflection. For Thomas Aquinas, Jesus is not meant so much to be worshiped as followed, or better, *shared in, participated in*. Thomas loved and commented upon the Gospel of John, which contains those beautifully organic descriptions of the relation between Christ and his disciples: "I am the vine, you are the branches" (John 15:5), and "Those who eat my flesh and drink my blood have eternal life" (John 6:54). Christ does not want to be admired as a metaphysical wonder or exception; on the contrary, he wants to be eaten and drunk, consumed, taken on. He wants to be source of life for the rest of us, to give what has been given to him. In a word, he longs, precisely as a human being, to be a model of love and receptivity to the divine source of his being. For Aquinas, the grace-filled humanity of the savior sets up a sort of field of force in which the whole of humanity can be transformed and energized. The human Christ's habitual grace, his fundamental orientation to God, is the exemplar and power by which all Christians are turned toward the ever greater revealer. The grace, found in excessive quantity in the humanity of Jesus, overflows, as it were, into the minds and hearts of those who are grasped by God through him.

There is a lovely passage in question 8, article 3, where Thomas speaks of the all-embracing quality of Christ's grace as head of the Church, as exemplar for the entire race:

> For first and principally, he is the head of such as are united to him by glory; second, of those who are actually united to him by charity; third, of those who are actually united to him by faith; fourth, of those who are united to him merely in potentiality, which is not yet reduced to act, yet will be reduced to act according to divine predestination.[23]

Jesus Christ is the mediator of the divine power for those who are already in full union with God, those in glory; for those on earth who are currently at one with God through faith and love; and even for those who are not now with God but who nevertheless long for union. The ecstasy of the human Christ is the mode of

---

22. Bernard of Clairvaux, *Sermons on the Song of Songs*, in *Selected Works*, ed. J. Farina, trans. G.R. Evans (Mahwah, NJ: Paulist, 1987), 212.

23. *Summa theologiae* 3.8.3.

access to the divine power for those at all levels of the spiritual life: for those who have already "tasted and seen" and for those who remain in various ways hungry.

In his response to the first objection in this third article, Thomas addresses himself to a problem that is quite contemporary—namely, whether Christ is the exemplar, the head, for all people. The objector maintains that Jesus cannot be the head of those who are unbaptized and hence outside of the Church that is the Body of Christ. In answer, Thomas says that even the unbaptized, though not actually in the Church, are yet potentially so inasmuch as they long for salvation. In some ways anticipating Karl Rahner's theory of anonymous Christianity, Thomas implies that all human beings, basically longing for the coming together of divine and human love that has in fact occurred in Christ, are, implicitly or explicitly, formed according to the icon of Jesus the Messiah.[24] Christ is, for all, the unifying and organizing power, the *imago* of divine-human union that all people long to realize in themselves. This is not a type of Christian imperialism; rather, it is a wager that what has appeared in Christ—the shared ecstasy of God and the human—will indeed prove captivating, fascinating, entrancing to any person of any cultural background.

In order to understand with greatest clarity this alluring play between the human and divine in Jesus, we have to turn to the eighteenth question of the *tertia pars*, dealing with the unity of wills in the interior life of Christ. In the course of this discussion, Thomas spells out the dynamic that is at the core of his entire theological and spiritual project: exactly *how* human and divine *excessus* (ecstasy or self-surrender) come together in a mutually illuminating fashion. To grasp this is to learn how to live a life in imitation of Christ.

In the first article of question 18, Aquinas distances himself from the so-called monothelite position of Apollinaris, the view that in Christ there is only one divine will, and he unambiguously affirms the classical orthodox view that there are, in fact, two wills, divine and human, in Jesus. If in Christ God has assumed an integral human nature, it must follow, says Thomas, that he has "assumed" a fully constituted human will. Once again, the humanity of Jesus is not a vague front for his divinity, not simply the form under which divine power presented itself. On the contrary, Jesus is to the center of his being a play and tension between the created and the uncreated, including and especially at the level of will, of desire.

Now, as is often the case in Thomas' texts, it is in the back-and-forth movement of objection and response that this baldly stated position is fleshed out.

---

24. For his theory of anonymous Christianity, see Karl Rahner, "Anonymous and Explicit Faith," trans. David Morland, in *Theological Investigations* (New York: Seabury, 1979), 16:52–78.

The first objector maintains that the will is the first mover or "first commander" in whoever wills. But in Christ, he continues, the divine will was supreme, since everything human in Jesus was moved by that will. Thus, it follows that, de facto, whatever was proper to the human will in Jesus was swallowed up, overwhelmed by, the divine will. Indeed, he seems to imply, how could a will that is *perfectly* subordinate and subservient, that is wholly transparent to a higher power, possess any integrity of its own?

Aquinas' response to this commonsensical objection is worthy of careful study:

> Whatever was in the human nature of Christ was moved at the bidding of the divine will; yet it does not follow that in Christ there was no movement of the will proper to human nature, for the good wills of other saints are moved by God's will. . . . For although the will cannot be inwardly moved by any creature, yet it can be moved inwardly by God.[25]

Thomas grants that the human will of Christ was totally subordinate to the divine will, but he refuses to admit that such passivity amounted to a blotting out of Christ's human freedom. In defense of this rather peculiar claim, Thomas offers the observation that though the created will cannot, in its freedom, be moved inwardly by any creature, it can be so moved by God. But how is this possible? What is the difference between manipulation by a creature and manipulation by God?

In answer, Aquinas refers us to question 105 of the *prima pars*, where he discusses the presence of God in the will for the first time. There the Dominican master argues that God is irresistibly present to the will precisely as the ground of the will, precisely as the ultimate good that is always desired in any concrete act of the will.[26] Whenever a person makes a particular choice—whether it is the trivial decision to see this movie rather than that or a significant decision to pursue a given career—she is, says Thomas, implicitly desiring her ultimate happiness. All individual acts of the will rest upon, depend upon, the final and all-embracing desire for the good itself—which is none other than God. For example, in deciding to paint, the artist is seeking the ultimate good that is the beautiful itself; in choosing to take on a particular case, the lawyer is motivated (at least ideally!) by the love for the final value that is justice itself. To be fully itself, the will must give itself radically to this good, must be totally conformed to it. Therefore, God's "manipulation" of the will is tantamount not to the

---

25. *Summa theologiae* 3.18.1 ad. 1.
26. *Summa theologiae* 1.105.4.

destruction of the will but to its preservation. The will finds itself in surrendering to the good that is its ground and end and *raison d'être*. Authentic freedom for the human will consists, paradoxically, in enslaving itself to the divine power.

This is but a particular example of the general principle of what I will call noncompetitiveness between God and creatures. Because God is not a being in the world—that is to say, not something that exists alongside of other creatures—God can enter into the being of a finite thing with great intimacy and *without compromising the independence and integrity of that thing*. A creature can enter into the reality of another creature only in an *aggressive* and domineering sense, the former forcing the latter as it were to cede something of itself. To give a perhaps crude example, a tiger assimilates, takes into itself, the being of the antelope only through attack, destruction, and finally ingestion; the antelope has to cede its being to the *aggressor*, "becoming" the tiger only through total loss of identity. What Aquinas implies in this entire discussion is that God does not operate in this way; when God *becomes* a creature, the creature is raised up, not diminished, brought to fulfillment, not overcome.

Now, for Thomas the great paradigm and archetype of this nonaggressive, noncompetitive relationship between God and the world is the Incarnation itself: the two natures of Christ are present together in a personal unity, but neither is mixed or mingled or confused with the other, neither is compromised or overwhelmed by the other. And therefore the absolute control of the divine will over the human will in Christ is not a negation of Jesus' humanity but rather an elevation of it. The human will of Jesus is perfectly aligned with, totally dependent on, and completely surrendered to the divine will.

It was Anselm of Canterbury who gave classic expression to this principle when he reminded us that authentic freedom is not to hover sovereignly above the "yes" and the "no," but instead to be bound to "yes" alone.[27] To be torn between yes and no is, says Anselm, to be caught in the intolerable situation of the sinner. What appears to be freedom in the eyes of the world—the ability to choose this or that, good or evil—is in fact the deepest type of slavery. God's freedom is equivalent to God's fidelity in love, to his capacity to say nothing but yes, and our freedom is found in imitation of that divine liberty. For Thomas, we know this in light of Jesus Christ, the human being fully alive and fully free precisely in his complete openness to, and passivity before, the will of God.

---

27. See Anselm, *On Free Will*, trans. Ralph McInerny, chap. 1, "That the Power of Sinning Does Not Pertain to Free Will," in *Anselm of Canterbury: The Major Works*, ed. Brian Davies and G.R. Evans (Oxford: Oxford University Press, 1998), 175–176.

And thus, once again, our principle is confirmed: the *excessus,* the ecstasy or self-surrender, of Christ is what allows the *excessus* of God to manifest itself in him. And we who participate in the energy of Christ, we who are "kissed with the kiss of his mouth," are those who become most fully ourselves in a similar act of obedience and self-transcendence. The great tragedy of sin is forgetting this mutual ecstasy and imagining God and oneself as self-contained rivals and competitors. In the heart of the sinner is the conviction that letting go of himself is tantamount to losing himself. The illusory sense is that the more the sinner affirms herself over and against God, the more she asserts the independence of her mind and will, the more she finds herself. What is disclosed in Christ is the unmasking of that illusion: the humanity of Jesus is elevated and fulfilled precisely in Jesus' willingness to be an *instrumentum* (instrument) of the ever-greater God, precisely in surrender to the authority of the Father. What the humanity of Jesus shows us is that leaving the confines of one's puny ego and allowing the *excessus* of God to come to birth is the only route to self-discovery.

Conclusion

At the very beginning of the *Summa,* Thomas told us that he would speak of God from the standpoint of the experience of being lifted out of himself by God's own self-disclosure. He would speak of the power that moves him and shakes him, turning him toward the infinite and thus to his own salvation. And toward the end of his masterpiece, Aquinas explicitly tells us where and how that salvation takes place: in the mutual ecstasy that is the God-human, Jesus Christ. In him we see simultaneously the grace that saves and the stance of the saved.

Thus, the icon, the image, in whose light Thomas Aquinas' teaching should be read is that of Christ, the meeting of divine and human self-forgetting. Whenever Thomas speaks of God, he describes not some philosophical abstraction, but the ever-greater, ever-more-surprising power that appeared in Jesus the Christ. And consequently, whenever he speaks of God, he implicitly describes the *proper human stance vis-à-vis God,* that attitude of obedience, openness, and self-transcending love that alone allows the fullness of the divine to emerge. As a theologian of revelation, Thomas is a doctor of the soul, a spiritual master trying to show the reader how to see God with the eyes of Christ, to touch God with the hands of Christ, to feel God with the heart of Christ.

Martin Luther was sharply critical of Thomas and other scholastic thinkers for theologizing about God *in se* (in himself) without reference to God's embrace of the human race, God's activity *pro nobis* (for us).[28] Our reading of Thomas' texts on revelation and Christology show that this charge is unfair. Aquinas is not interested in God in himself but only in that God who seizes us, turns us around, and frankly shocks us by the strangeness and unpredictability of his love shown forth in Christ.

Given this assumption concerning Thomas' method, I think it is possible to rediscover an enormous spiritual vitality in his seemingly arid texts. As we have seen, the Thomistic style is marked by the back-and-forth movement of objection and response, the dialectical play of question and answer. If Thomas' final purpose is to lure the reader into the attitude of Christ, then the objections can be appreciated not simply as intellectual counterpositions but as *spiritual counterpositions.* The objector is cleverly resisting the demanding spiritual attitude that Thomas is trying to inculcate, and the soul master, Aquinas, in his responses, is patiently tracking him down, correcting him, putting him back on the beam. An incorrect understanding of God is always in correlation with an improper *human attitude* toward God, with an un-Christlike perspective.

Why are there so many questions, so many articles, so many objections and responses in the *Summa*? One might respond: because there are so many ways that the sinful soul can evade the call to Christlike obedience and openness of heart. Like Ignatius and John of the Cross, Thomas is extremely sensitive to the darkness of the spirit, to the labyrinthine ways of sin, and, again like those two great masters of the soul, he has the patience and the love required to seek out the sinner despite all obstacles. Thomas will not rest until his reader is lured into wonder and ecstasy.

---

28. Catherine Mowry LaCugna describes Luther's objection to Thomist and scholastic theology in similar terms in *God for Us: The Trinity and Christian Life* (Chicago: HarperOne, 1973), 144. For two primary-source examples of Luther's objection to the scholastic methodology that St. Thomas supposedly exemplified, see his *Disputation against Scholastic Theology* and *The Babylonian Captivity of the Church,* in *Martin Luther's Basic Theological Writings,* 3rd ed., ed. Timothy F. Lull and William R. Russell (Minneapolis, MN: Fortress, 2012), 3–7, 196–224, esp. 206.

Chapter Two

THE STRANGENESS
OF GOD

The God who comes to us in Jesus Christ, who lifts us up beyond ourselves and moves us to salvation, the God of ecstatic self-offering, the God whose outreach of love is greater than we can think or imagine, is very strange. That, it seems to me, is a valid one-sentence summary of Thomas Aquinas' doctrine of God. What Thomas endeavors to say in his hundreds of pages on God is really quite simple: God is uncanny. Whatever you can say or think or assert concerning God falls infinitely short of who God actually is. Indeed, the best and finally the only response to the divine power is silence, the silence of awe and reverence and hope. In a sense, Ludwig Wittgenstein's famous adage, "Whereof one cannot speak, thereof one must be silent," is applicable to Thomas' teaching on God.[1] Though he writes voluminously on the divine existence and nature, Thomas never tells us anything about God; he only tells us what God is not. And this pious silence, this reverential negativity, is, as always, in service of Aquinas' spiritual project: to blow open the mind of his readers, to tantalize their imagination, to stir their hearts, to orient them more and more to that elusive power disclosed in Christ, that unimaginable love that alone can satisfy.

What I want to do in the course of this chapter is to follow Thomas Aquinas as he performs this dual task of naming God and directing the soul. We will consider first two of the famous "arguments" for the existence of God and see how Thomas uses them to lead his readers into a richer appreciation of the revealing God. Next, we shall look at Thomas' presentation of the various attributes of God—simplicity, goodness, presence in the world, eternity, immutability, knowledge, will, love—and see, first, why these are proper descriptions of the God of Jesus Christ and, second, how these descriptions of the divine indirectly

------

1. Ludwig Wittgenstein, *Tractatus Logico-Philosophicus* 7, trans. Charles Kay Ogden (London: Kegan Paul, 1922), 189.

change the minds and hearts of his readers, moving them into a more Christlike stance of obedience and love.

The "Proofs" for God's Existence

We approach Thomas' arguments for God's existence with some trepidation because they are among the most famous and talked-about texts in the history of theology. Oceans of ink have been spilled in the attempt to explain, bolster, attack, undermine, or defend these "proofs" that God exists. Interestingly, both believers and nonbelievers have defended them—and both believers and nonbelievers have denied them. For some, they provide a rational foundation for religious belief, and for others they represent the pathetic and arrogant human attempt to capture God in a net of concepts and logical necessities. For some, they furnish a purely reasonable ground for accepting the existence of God, a justification beyond all of the petty disputes of the various faith traditions, and for others they are a hopeless muddle of outmoded ideas and questionable logical moves.

It is my conviction that both the ardent defenders and the passionate critics of these proofs have, for the most part, misread them. When they are seen, by either their proponents or opponents, as the foundation upon which Thomas builds his theology, they are given an importance that they do not merit. We have seen that there is only one foundation for the theological project of Aquinas—namely, the revelatory act by which God speaks his ever-greater and ever-more-surprising love in Jesus Christ. Whatever else follows in the *Summa* is an elaboration and explication of that event, a showing forth in various ways of the light and power of Christ. Thomas does not begin his theology with the philosophical proofs; rather, he transforms them and then uses them according to the principle that he established in the first question of the *Summa*. These various *ways* in which philosophers have proven the existence of God are utilized by our spiritual master as *manuductiones*, leadings by the hand, methods by which the fallen mind is led to an appreciation of the God of revelation. More precisely, in light of Jesus Christ, they become ways of orienting the reader to the all-embracing power of God, means of showing that all aspects of one's life ultimately find their origin and source in the divine love that Jesus disclosed.

It is very instructive that Thomas refers to the five demonstrations that he offers not as proofs but as *viae*, ways. As we have seen, this word *via* is used at the beginning of the *tertia pars* to designate the way to God who is Jesus Christ. They are paths that the spiritual master lays out in order to lead the reader finally to *the path* that alone discloses the God who is really God. It should be abundantly clear that Thomas does not formulate these arguments in the spirit of Voltaire or Descartes—that is to say, as a rationalist unconvinced of God's existence and endeavoring to prove or disprove it to his satisfaction. The theologian who lays out these ways is someone who has already been grasped by the God of Jesus Christ, someone already on the way and now attempting to lure others onto that path.

With these remarks in mind, let us turn to that *via*, the argument from motion, which Thomas calls the "first and more manifest."[2] Aquinas tells us that it is certain and evident to our senses that some things in the world move. Following Aristotle, Thomas takes the term "motion" in the very broad sense of transition or change, in his words, the "reduction of something from potentiality to actuality," from nonbeing to being.[3] Whatever is in the process of changing must be in potency, but whatever causes the change must be in act, since nothing gives what it does not have. From this it follows, says Thomas, that nothing can move itself, since any self-mover would have to be potential and actual at the same time and in the same respect. To use Aquinas' own example, the log, which is potentially hot, cannot warm itself, but must *be changed* by the fire that is actually hot. Nothing, finally, is autonomous in its *motus* (motion); all change points beyond itself to an exterior cause.

Now, if that which causes a particular change is itself being changed, it, too, must be changed by another, and that, if moved, by another again. But a chain of moved movers cannot proceed to infinity,

> because then there would be no first mover, and, consequently, no other mover; seeing that subsequent movers move only inasmuch as they are put in motion by the first mover; as the staff moves only because it is put in motion by the hand. Therefore it is necessary to arrive at a first mover, put in motion by no other; and this everyone understands to be God.[4]

To avoid misunderstanding, it is very important to note that this negation of an infinite series of moved movers should not be interpreted in a deist sense, as if Aquinas were demonstrating the existence of a temporally first mover at the "beginning of time." Thomas' demonstration says absolutely nothing, for

---

2. Thomas Aquinas, *Summa theologiae* 1.2.3.

3. *Summa theologiae* 1.2.3.

4. *Summa theologiae* 1.2.3.

example, about the origin of the universe, about the "big bang" theory of cosmic generation, or about the historical beginnings of the world.

What he does in fact deny is the possibility of an infinite series of moved movers in which each agent depends *here and now* on the influence of the agent just above it in the hierarchy. If that sort of chain were indefinite, if there were no "first" element in it, there would be no movement *now*, no change at the bottom of the series. The first mover to which Thomas concludes is not a distant force, in either a physical or chronological sense; on the contrary, it is a power that is here and now intimately involved in the movement of things in the world.

What coloring does this familiar and classical demonstration take on if we read it not so much as a rational starting point for Thomas' theology, but rather as an explication of the great event of revelation in Jesus Christ? What would this proof look like if we read it as Thomas intended it, as a "leading by the hand," a means of guiding us more surely into the mystery of God? At the outset, it seems as though we are dealing with an objective, even rather scientific, analysis of the various motions and transitions discernible in the universe. However, we must be attentive to the centrality of the theme of movement in the overall structure of the *Summa*, especially in the questions that inaugurate each major division. As we saw in question 1 of the *prima pars*, the whole point of God's revealing activity is to move, redirect, and reorient fallen human beings, to set them on the path that leads to God. And, as was specified in the opening question of the *tertia pars*, the purpose of the Incarnation is to lift human beings up, to move them from a consideration of the world to a vision of the divine. And acting as a hinge between revelation and Christology is the first question of the second part, wherein Thomas explores the final end of the human person. In the brief introductory section to that question, Aquinas announces his purpose: to consider the ultimate goal of human life and "those things through which the human being can come to this end."

In short, each major section of Thomas' masterwork is conditioned by the problem of the *movement* of the human being toward God, the orientation of the sinner to salvation. One could argue that this theme of spiritual *motus* is the motif that dominates the whole of the *Summa theologiae*. Thus, it seems hardly accidental that, in the "first and more manifest" way to prove the existence of God, Thomas begins with the phenomenon of motion. What he begins with, I would argue, is what concerns him throughout the *Summa*—namely, the errant and correct movements of the human being. Without denying the properly cosmological dimension of the demonstration, what we see here primarily is an analysis of the spiritual "motion" toward or away from God. As always, Aquinas is endeavoring here to move people onto the path who is Jesus Christ.

If spiritual change or movement is the primary focus of this argument, then Thomas' careful denial of self-movement in the first half of the demonstration takes on an interesting anthropological significance. In denying that something can change itself, that it can set itself on its own path, Thomas negates the sinful drive toward radical autonomy, toward self-direction. The human being who moves himself has become his own God and has simply identified the ultimate motive force with his own mind and will, his own ego. The great medieval dictum *omne quod movetur, ab alio movetur* (whatever is moved is moved by another) can be read in this context not so much as a principle of physics but as a piece of spiritual wisdom, urging the sinner to let go of the illusion of self-direction and to surrender to the influence of another.[5] We recall that the basic dynamic of the humanity of Christ was the refusal to cling to his own mind and will and the concomitant surrender to the direction of the Other who is the Father.

But there is more to Thomas' proof than the denial of self-movement, because there is a greater range to the sinner's strategy. The one in rebellion against God might let go of himself, admitting that he cannot move himself, only then to surrender his life to another finite reality, to money or power or prestige, to a political party or to a charismatic leader. In terms of Thomas' demonstration, he would then be giving the direction of his life over to a "moved mover." Thus, what Aquinas shows in the second half of the proof is that all the motion and causal agency in the world must finally come under the influence of a mover that is outside of the web of finite things, that is not simply one more element in the chain of finite causes. In insisting on the impossibility of an infinite series of changed changers, our spiritual master compels the sinner to look, for the final direction of her life, to a power that is not simply "another being in the world," to an authority that "moves" but that is not itself "moved." It is only this reality that effectively lifts human beings out of self-complacency and orients them to a truly transcendent end.

It is very interesting to me that Thomas concludes his proof with the tag line: "and this [the first mover] everyone understands to be God."[6] We have seen who God is for Thomas Aquinas: the alluring, ever-greater, and transcendent power that draws us out beyond ourselves to a fulfilling and beatific vision of beauty. In identifying the "first mover" with God, Thomas reveals the essentially spiritual and mystical élan of this proof; he shows us that the demonstration has to do not so much with cosmology as with the geography of the soul.

---

5. For discussion of the principle *omne quod movetur, ab alio movetur* see James A. Weisheipl, "The Principle *Omne quod movetur ab alio movetur* in Medieval Physics," *Isis* 56, no. 1 (1965): 26–45.

6. *Summa theologiae* 1.2.3.

In a sense, the spiritual dynamic of this demonstration is similar to that found in the tenth book of the *Confessions* of St. Augustine, wherein the saint interrogates nature, all the beauty and splendor of finite creation, in search of God. The "sea and the deeps . . . the creeping things . . . the winds that blow . . . the heavens, the sun, the moon, the stars" join in unison and deny their divinity: "We are not your God; seek higher."[7] In other words, God, the ultimate good of one's life, cannot be discovered in anything that is merely finite, anything that can be found in the world. In the more sober language of Aquinas, the soul is urged to look for God neither in himself (no self-movement) nor in the things of the world, no matter how impressive (no infinite regress of moved movers), but rather only in that power that is fundamentally transcendent, only in the unmoved mover.

There is something implied in this proof that is of great comfort to us sinners. Thomas shows that whatever is in motion is in fact *always and inevitably moved by God*. In terms of our spiritual reading, this means that whoever is moving toward her end, toward her happiness, is finally being lured by God, whether she knows it or not. Even if the sinner is convinced that he or some other finite power is his first mover, in point of fact, God is his first mover. Toward the beginning of the *Summa*, Thomas tells us that all people, in desiring to be happy, are implicitly desiring God, since God alone is our final happiness.[8] To be sure, one can live under the illusion that ultimate happiness is something other than God, but the desire for happiness itself is proof that God is subtly at work in the soul of even the most hardened sinner. There is no move possible in human life that is not, in some inchoate, groping way, a move under the influence of God. In his autobiography, *The Seven Storey Mountain*, Thomas Merton describes the various paths he took that led him, it seemed, away from God.[9] But from the vantage point of his later years, he saw that each of these errant journeys was in fact animated and touched by a deep hunger for the divine, and thus that God was mysteriously at work even at the least God-filled moments. Such an insight is the spiritual heart of the first "way."

With this more soulful reading of the first proof in mind, let us turn now to the notoriously complex and puzzling third argument for God's existence, the proof from possibility and necessity. I am convinced that this argument can come to life and speak powerfully to the spirit if we but read it as a further illumination of the revelation contained in Christ. It is worthwhile to follow the

7. Augustine, *Confessions* 10.6, trans. F.J. Sheed, ed. Michael P. Foley (Park Ridge, IL: Word on Fire Classics, 2017), 236.

8. *Summa theologiae* 1-2.2.8.

9. Thomas Merton, *The Seven Storey Mountain* (Park Ridge, IL: Word on Fire Classics, 2017).

sinuous movement of this proof in order to appreciate the delicacy of the spiritual direction involved.

Thomas begins by asserting that we find things in the world that are possible to be and not to be, things that, in more technical language, are susceptible to generation and corruption.[10] Again following Aristotle, Aquinas understands generation and corruption to be the two types of substantial change—that is to say, the processes by which things radically come into being and pass out of being. Thus, for example, wood is corrupted into ash and plants are generated from soil and sun. Thomas' point is that whatever has this capacity to come into existence and pass out of existence cannot be described as necessary but only as possible.

It is at this juncture that Aquinas' argument takes a rather curious turn. It is urged that whatever is possible, capable of being or nonbeing, "at some time is not."[11] What Thomas implies here is that the merely possible carries with it a sort of heritage of nonbeing, an irresistible tendency toward nonexistence. The merely possible is that which is constantly under the threat of falling out of being. And thus, he continues, if everything were of this type, there would be nothing in existence now, the internal "clocks" of all things having run down, the tendency toward nonbeing in all having been realized.

> Therefore not all beings are merely possible, but there must exist something the existence of which is necessary. But every necessary thing either has its necessity caused by another, or not. Now it is impossible to go on to infinity in necessary things which have their necessity caused by another. . . . Therefore we cannot but postulate the existence of some being having of itself its own necessity, and not receiving it from another. . . . And this all men speak of as God.[12]

Since it cannot be the case that all things are merely possible, there must exist, says Thomas, at least some being that is necessary. It is most important not to jump to the conclusion that in claiming this he has already arrived at the existence of God. All he means at this point is that there must be something in the universe that does not come into or pass out of being, something stable enough to lend a degree of stability to the ever-changing realm of possible things. For Thomas, as for Aristotle before him, planets, stars, and angels would all qualify as such necessary realities, since they are not generated or corrupted.[13]

---

10. *Summa theologiae* 1.2.3.
11. *Summa theologiae* 1.2.3.
12. *Summa theologiae* 1.2.3.
13. See, for instance, Thomas Aquinas, *Summa contra Gentiles* 2.30; *Summa theologiae* 1.50.5 ad. 3.

These could be the final and unchanging powers that serve to anchor and renew the world over time.

Thus, at the conclusion of the first section of the proof, Aquinas has established that there are at least two levels of reality: the everyday dimension of fleeting reality and the more ethereal dimension of stable reality. But it is at this point that Thomas makes the move to the sheerly unique and mysterious being that is God. This second dimension of necessary things derives its necessity, its stability of being, from a final, ultimate cause that has its necessity from itself, that, in other words, exists through the aid or influence of no other reality. And it is this being that in turn grants stability to the whole of the universe. It is only this sheerly independent, utterly necessary reality, this power that simply *is* without qualification, that "all people call God."[14]

Now, I realize that my reader might be wondering how this arcane and convoluted demonstration could ever qualify as spiritual direction. Once more we must keep in mind the basic attitude of Aquinas: with these proofs he is trying to guide the reader to an acceptance of the God who has spoken in Jesus Christ. With this in mind, let us open up this proof. As the first demonstration began with the theme of movement toward God, this third argument begins with a very contemporary theme: the instability and uncertainty of being, more precisely of our human being. We come into existence without being consulted—indeed, as Heidegger indicates, we are "thrown" into being.[15] And we are continually haunted by the unavoidable fact of our mortality, by the inevitable onset of the substantial change that Thomas calls corruption. The conviction that we are thrown into being and will eventually be wrenched out of it persuades us that we are not self-explanatory, not self-sufficient. And this conviction is one not of the intellect alone but rather one that seeps into our blood and bones, one that frightens us and determines our actions in ways both conscious and unconscious. This mere possibility of our being is what effectively disabuses us of the illusory notion that we are our own masters, that our existence provides its own ground. Just as the first proof begins with the demonstration that we do not move or determine ourselves, so the third argument begins with the disquieting observation that we do not exist by and through ourselves. Thus, the first move in Thomas' third way, read from the spiritual perspective, is just this decentering of the ego: the human being must look to what is other in order to find the ultimate ground and support for his existence.

---

14. *Summa theologiae* 1.2.3 (translation mine).
15. Martin Heidegger, *Being and Time*, trans. John Macquarrie and Edward Robinson (New York: Harper Perennial, 2008), 174–225.

However, this decentering of the ego is but a first step, and hence the demonstration continues. Having moved off of his ego, having accepted the fact of his own insufficiency, a person could spontaneously seek the support that he craves in another finite reality, in another corruptible thing. He might flee to money, to power, to material things, to the affection of another—expecting these to provide the ground for his life. It is just such a move that Thomas precludes in insisting that all corruptibles, all those things that are destined to fall into nonbeing, cannot possibly be the ultimate stabilizing force. Behind the metaphysical language, the spiritual master is urging his readers not to sink their lives into the passing things of the world.

The fleetingness and insubstantiality of the realm of generation and corruption led Thomas, as we saw, to postulate the existence of another dimension of being—namely, the necessary. Alongside of merely corruptible things, there must be some realities that have a greater stability, a greater permanence and power. In these necessary beings—be they heavenly bodies or angels or souls—one can find some anchor of stability in the swirling incertitude of finitude. However, Thomas insists that even these permanent things are not the final source and ground of the universe, since they derive their necessity from that which is necessary through itself. When read from our spiritual standpoint, this clarification is of decisive importance. In seeking the path that leads to fulfillment, a person can have made the necessary preliminary moves of decentering the ego and eschewing corruptible things and nevertheless fall into the trap of basing his life upon one of the powers that is permanent and yet less than God. In the context of our experience, many realities could be described as necessary in Thomas' sense: ideals, political convictions, national identity, racial consciousness, heroic achievement, etc., in short, all those principles that perdure across time and that are fundamentally immune to the ravages of corruption. These great "powers and principalities" can be easily grasped as absolutes—precisely by those spiritual travelers who are relatively accomplished, who have passed beyond the first two temptations. One thinks readily of certain political revolutionaries—Robespierre, Lenin, Mao Zedong—who have transcended their narrow self-interest, who have left behind the corruptible values of wealth and sensuality, who in some ways led lives of heroic self-sacrifice, but who in the end accept as their god a political/cultural program. It is to such as these that the last section of the third proof is directed. Even the permanent things in the world, even those powers that endure across time, even those great ideals of the human condition *are not the ultimate or final necessity; they are not God*. Whatever good and permanence they have is derived from the sheer goodness and permanence of Being itself.

There is, if you will, a sort of triple "shaking" that happens in this proof. Seized by the God of Jesus Christ, the God of ever-greater and unsurpassable power, Thomas Aquinas wants to put his readers on the path that leads to that God. In order to enter onto the *way*, the disciples must first be shaken out of their own self-complacency, their tendency to cling to their *egos*; then they must be shaken out of their immersion in the passing things of the world; and finally they must be stirred out of their allegiance to the mighty and permanent powers that are yet less than God. Each step in the proof represents a reorienting intervention of the spiritual director, a call continually to look higher.

This theme of the contingency and danger of being human is central to the work of the great twentieth-century Protestant thinker Paul Tillich. For the German theologian, finitude itself is a condition that is always under the threat of nonbeing and finally destined to succumb to the onslaught of the powers of nonexistence.[16] To be human is to live with the startling and disquieting awareness of this fact. At the heart of the spiritual quest, for Tillich, is the desire to find the "courage to be"—that is to say, to discover that ground upon which one can finally stand, that power of being that provides stability even under the threat of nonbeing.[17] To my mind, this third argument of Thomas Aquinas is, in a similar way, a quest for the courage to be. Like Tillich, Thomas signals to his readers the precariousness of human existence and then orients them to the one source that can conquer the fear of being finite.

I find a connection between the sort of spiritual direction in Thomas' third proof and that used by Jesus himself in John's account of the woman at the well (John 4:1–42). We recall that in John's narrative the Samaritan woman comes to the well seeking water. There she confronts Jesus, who reminds her that she has returned again and again to that well but has never been satisfied. In spiritual terms, this rhythm of drinking and becoming thirsty again is evocative of the trap of concupiscent desire. When a person seeks to fill her infinite hunger for God with something finite, something "corruptible," she will never be satisfied and will return to the source repeatedly but each time will be more frustrated, more weary. Jesus tells the woman at the well not to seek the center of her life in the perishable and passing things of the finite realm, but rather to seek "living water," the power of the eternal. In Thomistic terms, Jesus is drawing the woman from the corruptible to the necessary.

---

16. Paul Tillich, *Systematic Theology* (Chicago: The University of Chicago Press, 1951–1963), 1:196.

17. Paul Tillich, *The Courage to Be* (New Haven, CT: Yale University Press, 1952).

But, as Thomas himself implies, there is the danger that one could become fixated at the level of the necessary powers without penetrating to that which is necessary through itself—namely, God. The Samaritan woman faces the same danger. Having been lured by Christ away from the well and having acknowledged that Jesus is a prophet, she asks him whether appropriate worship takes place in the Jerusalem temple, as the Jews say, or on the holy mountain, as the Samaritans have it. She is seeking the center and orientation of her life not in the properly eternal reality of God but rather in a particular religious tradition. In terms of Thomas' demonstration, she is wondering whether to anchor her life in one of those necessary powers, one of those great principalities that falls, nevertheless, short of God. Jesus' answer to this question is magnificent: "Woman, believe me, the hour is coming when you will worship the Father neither on this mountain nor in Jerusalem. . . . God is spirit, and those who worship must worship in spirit and truth" (John 4:21, 24). In other words, the divine is not a reality in this world, not something that can be caught in the categories of finitude, not "this" or "that," but is rather spirit that transcends even those "necessary" powers that are the great religious traditions. Jesus "shakes" the Samaritan woman out of her immersion in the corruptible goods of the world and then out of her allegiance to even those noble "necessities" that are religions—in order to open her mind and heart to the uncontrollable, unlimited mystery that is God. Thomas Aquinas imitates his Master in the subtle soul work of the third argument.

Having read the first and third proofs from a more Christological and spiritual perspective, we can see that Thomas uses these demonstrations to shake and to reorient his readers. He wants to show us that none of us is our own master, and that finally, in the words of one of the Sunday Prefaces from the Roman liturgy, "in you [O God] we live and move and have our being" (cf. Acts 17:28).[18] With these "ways," Aquinas leads us by the hand to an experience of the all-embracing and all-grounding power that discloses itself in Jesus Christ. In these proofs, he shows us that in the roots of our being we are in relation to a reality that is utterly unlike the finite and contingent things of the world, that we are in the saving grasp of something stranger than we can possibly imagine.

---

18. "Preface VI of the Sundays in Ordinary Time," in *Roman Missal* (ICEL, 2010).

The Simple Reality

As I hinted in the opening paragraphs of this chapter, the doctrine of God that Thomas develops in the *Summa* is really an anti-doctrine—that is to say, a consistent display of what God is not. Like a sculptor, Aquinas carefully carves away from our notion of God anything that smacks of the creaturely, the finite, the particular. His theology is redolent of the spirit of the Old Testament prophets who were concerned above all with overcoming the danger of idolatry. Speaking boldly from the heart of God himself, Isaiah cries out: "For as the heavens are higher than the earth, so are my ways higher than your ways and my thoughts than your thoughts" (Isa. 55:9). Similarly, Thomas Aquinas stubbornly battles the sinful tendency to draw the infinite and unsearchable power of God into the customary categories of thought. What informs the entire Thomistic analysis of God is, as always, the revelation contained in the Incarnation: the God who was capable of such an act of love must be, to use Anselm's phrase, "that than which nothing greater can be thought."[19] It is particularly intriguing to watch the play between objections and responses in this part of the *Summa*. Taking the position of the sinner, the "objectors" continually try to domesticate, to finitize, the divine power, turning it into something that can be easily manipulated or avoided. With his customary calm determination, Thomas corrects each of these mistakes, heals each of these wounds of the soul.

Having explored the nature of revelation in question 1 and having shown us the various "ways" to orient the heart to God in question 2, Thomas turns in question 3 to a consideration of the divine *simplicitas* (simplicity). This perhaps surprising "attribute" of God is for Thomas the most highly characteristic, the most distinctive. What God's simplicity entails, in a word, is that the divine is not any sort of being, any *particular instance* of being, but is rather the sheer act of existing itself. God is not this or that; God simply is. Thomas endeavors to show this simplicity through a *via remotionis* (a way of removing)—that is to say, through a negation of all those qualities and attributes that would make of God something like a creature.

He begins in the first two articles of question 3 by denying that God is a material body. Aquinas' basic argument here is simple: matter is by its nature malleable, changeable, potential—and we have already seen that God is the first unmoved mover, that reality which changes the world without itself being

---

19. Anselm, *Proslogion* 2–5, in *Anselm: Monologion and Proslogion*, trans. Thomas Williams (Indianapolis, IN: Hackett, 1996), 99–102.

changed. Therefore, God cannot be a body.[20] On the face of it, this can seem to be a rather banal theological remark, but it takes on greater power when we set it against the backdrop of the tradition of idolatry to which we alluded above. One of the gravest temptations faced by the biblical believer was precisely this tendency to transform the ungraspable divine power into something crudely finite, to reduce one's ultimate concern to the level of corruptible things. Interestingly, the material realm, for Thomas, is that dimension of being that can be moved or manipulated. To place God in the category of the material is thus far from a mere intellectual error; on the contrary, it is representative of a fundamentally perverse spiritual orientation: the desire to control the divine and hence to place oneself above God. Thus, in affirming that God is not a body Thomas is once more shedding light on that strange power that appeared in Christ, that revealing and saving God who cannot in principle be controlled or avoided, that power that demands of us nothing short of surrender. In a symbolic sense, all creatures must be embodied vis-à-vis the fully "spiritual" God—that is to say, malleable, passive, receptive.

It is in the fourth article of question 3 that Thomas makes one of the most important clarifications in the entire *Summa*, for it is in this article that he speaks of the identity of essence and existence in the God of Jesus Christ. In making this claim, Thomas states as baldly as he can the simpleness and sheer actuality of the God who has seized him. In medieval metaphysics, essence is the *quidditas* or "whatness" of a thing, that basic form or structure that determines what type of being something is. Existence, on the other hand, is the concrete "that-ness" of an object, the act of being by which, and because of which, a thing is. Now, in any imaginable finite reality, argues Thomas, there is a real distinction between essence and existence. This means, quite simply, that a finite being exists according to a *mode* or *type* of being. To put it more imaginatively, a limited thing is that whose act of existence is "poured" into a particular mold or structure of being that is its essence. I am not the sheer act of being; rather, I am a *human* being, something whose *esse* (act of to-be) has been "received" and "limited" by the essence principle of humanity. This real distinction between essence and being holds for the simplest microscopic particle as well as for the angel: despite the enormous difference between them, both are "beings," not Being itself.

But God exists in a radically different manner, since he is not any type of being at all. Thomas explains:

> Whatever a thing has besides its essence must be caused either by the constitu-
> ent principles of that essence . . . or by some exterior agent—as heat is caused

20. *Summa theologiae* 1.3.1.

in water by fire. Therefore, if the existence of a thing differs from its essence, this existence must be caused either by some exterior agent or by its essential principles. Now it is impossible for a thing's existence to be caused by its essential constituent principles, for nothing can be the sufficient cause of its own existence. . . . Therefore that thing, whose existence differs from its essence, must have its existence caused by another. But this cannot be true of God, because we call God the first efficient cause. Therefore it is impossible that in God His existence should differ from His essence.[21]

Thomas' argument here can be stated quite simply: that in which there is a distinction between essence and existence must receive its being from something else; God does not receive his being from something else; therefore, in God there is no distinction between essence and existence. As the "first" reality, as the unsurpassable power, God is that reality that depends upon nothing outside of itself. God exists simply because it is his nature to exist. By implication, all other realities must exist *in and through* God, as participants in the sheer actuality of the divine. All other things in the universe are purely dependent upon the uncaused and underived nature of God; all the created universe swims, as it were, in the ocean of the divine being.

In other of his writings, Thomas makes the beautiful connection between this more philosophical statement of the way God exists and the enigmatic self-definition of God found in the book of Exodus. When Moses speaks to the burning bush, asking the name of the mysterious power that had summoned him, God responds, "I Am Who I Am" (Exod. 3:14). For Thomas Aquinas, this strange answer is, paradoxically, of stunning clarity. What God reveals is that his essence (who I am) is identical to his existence (I am). In a sense, Moses had asked a question in line with the religious sensibility typical of his time: "Which god are you?" He wanted to know the specific name of this god who had called him in order to distinguish him from the myriad other gods. God's response implies that the true God is not one divinity among many, not one type of reality, not even the supreme being above all other things, but rather Being itself, that which is beyond any of the customary categories.

For Thomas, both the sacred name disclosed in Exodus and the description of God as the identity of essence and existence are expressions of the anti-idolatry principle. Both serve to fight off the sinful tendency to turn God into a god—that is to say, into *another being* with whom I may or may not be related. If God is the sheer act of being, then I *must* be in *relation to him*. If the divine existence

21. *Summa theologiae* 1.3.4.

is the air that I breathe and the environment in which I function, then I am, willy-nilly, in rapport with God. Even when running from God—as all of us sinners do to varying degrees—we are, despite our best efforts, living, moving, and having our being in him.

In his essay "The Two Types of Philosophy of Religion," Paul Tillich says that there are traditionally two ways to think of God, two ways to encounter God.[22] According to the first, we see God as fundamentally a stranger, a distant supreme being, with whom we struggle to become related. According to the second, God is met as the root and ground of our being, as the one who knows us long before we come to know him, as the one who has found us even as we begin to search for him. It is this second approach, thinks Tillich, that authentically speaks of the God disclosed in Christ Jesus. Thomas Aquinas would be in agreement with Tillich on this point. For Thomas, too, the Incarnation discloses the simple God who cannot be avoided, who cannot be set aside, "the fullness of him who fills all in all" (Eph. 1:23), and who therefore "has" us even when we want nothing to do with him. Like Tillich, Thomas wants to dismantle the mythology of a supreme being, the idolatrous view that places God and the world in opposition and competition.

In article 5 of question 3, Aquinas wonders whether God can be placed, like finite things, in a genus—that is to say, in a general category of existence.[23] Given the divine simplicity, the answer is in the negative: God cannot be grouped with other things in a particular type or placed under a more general logical umbrella. The question itself is intriguing: the one who imagines that God could be somehow categorized *must stand in a position superior to* God. Even if one were to say, for example, that God is the highest reality in the category of beings, God would still be known and controlled by the sovereign mind of the *categorizer*. The theologian confidently placing God in the right logical slot would subtly but undeniably be asserting his mastery of the divine—and this is nothing but the supreme fantasy of the sinful ego. When Moses asked God for his name, he was placing himself in a similar spiritual danger. And thus God's answer is a sort of Zen koan, a purposely puzzling and disconcerting remark designed to change the consciousness of the questioner. "I Am Who I Am" could be interpreted as a refusal to be caught in the trap of the question—and an attempt to challenge the presuppositions of the one who poses the question.

---

22. Paul Tillich, "The Two Types of Philosophy of Religion," in *Theology of Culture*, ed. Robert C. Kimball (Oxford: Oxford University Press, 1959), 10–29.

23. *Summa theologiae* 1.3.5.

The Goodness of God

Having shown that God, in his simplicity and perfection, is unlike any created reality, Thomas endeavors in question 6 to demonstrate that God is properly described as alluring. Once more the transition is not accidental. One could admit that God is perfect and, precisely in that admission, fall out of communion with God. Since the perfect one is overwhelming, unapproachable, infinitely above the level of the creature, it would be rather easy to feel at a distance from such a reality. One could honor God as perfect but not be the least bit captivated by or drawn to that perfection. On the contrary, one could respond to it in fear or with a terrible sense of unworthiness. In question 6, Thomas attempts to overcome these dangers by showing that the very perfection of God renders him good—that is to say, attractive, compelling, fascinating.

Following Aristotle, Aquinas relates goodness to desirability: we call "good" that which attracts us, that which awakens our desire.[24] But all things, Thomas tells us, want their own perfection, the full flowering of their natures.

> And the perfection and form of an effect consists in a certain likeness to the agent, since every agent makes its like; and hence the agent itself is desirable and has the nature of good. For the very thing which is desirable in it is the participation of its likeness.[25]

What we see here with great clarity is the Thomistic theme of the return to the source. There is, he implies, a sort of mirroring dynamic between cause and effect: the former produces its likeness in the latter, and the latter sees its exemplar in the former. The cause is the fullness from which the effect has come and to which it longs to "return" through imitation or participation. Thus, a child recognizes his parents and his culture—his causes—as exemplars, ideals that he longs to emulate, sources from which he desires to drink. Desire itself, Thomas insinuates, is awakened through a contemplation of these exemplary perfections.

> Therefore, since God is the first effective cause of all things, it is manifest that the aspect of good and of desirableness belong to him; and hence Dionysius attributes good to God as to the first efficient cause, saying that God is called good "as by whom all things subsist."[26]

---

24. *Summa theologiae* 1.6.1 obj. 2. See also Aristotle, *Nicomachean Ethics* 1.1.
25. *Summa theologiae* 1.6.1.
26. *Summa theologiae* 1.6.1. See also Pseudo-Dionysius, *The Divine Names* 4, in *Pseudo-Dionysius: The Complete Works*, trans. Colm Luibheid (New York: Paulist, 1987), 71–96.

Precisely as the all-embracing and all-grounding cause of finite reality, God must be named as supremely good. He is the perfect cause from which all effects have come forth and hence the fullness of being that all effects long to imitate. Since all created being is a reflection of God, God must be the exemplar, the icon, that the created realm desires to emulate. The perfection of any finite thing's being must be found in the pure perfection of the first and all-enveloping cause.

What I hope has emerged clearly in this argument is the dynamic character of God's goodness. God is called good inasmuch as he enters into the minds and hearts of his rational creatures, luring them to fullness of being. The divine perfection becomes a sort of magnetic force drawing the whole of the universe out of itself. Once more, we encounter the theme of ecstasy: the divine goodness is not an attribute to be admired from a distance; rather, it is the goal that awakens love and ecstatic loss of self in the smitten creature. One is meant not to be crushed or discouraged by the sheer greatness of God but to be enlivened and perfected by it. We recall that Thomas Aquinas, when speaking of the good God, is describing the power that has appeared in Jesus Christ, the power that overwhelms the creature while allowing it to remain true to itself. It is the misconception of the sinner to suppose that God's greatness is alienating or off-putting or even an excuse to resign oneself to one's own mediocrity. Whenever we strive for any good, we are, consciously or unconsciously, striving to attain something of the goodness of God.

God's Presence in the World

In question 8 of the first part of the *Summa*, Thomas addresses himself to the rather existential concern of whether God is really present in and to the world. Is the perfect, simple, and all-good God implicated in the everyday affairs of the created world, or is he a sheerly transcendent force? At this point in our discussion, we should be able to anticipate Thomas' answer: the God whose goodness, perfection, and simplicity are disclosed supereminently in the event of the Incarnation must be a God more than capable of lurking in the world. There has obviously been an enormous amount of ink spilled on this problem of God's relation to the universe. In my view, the subtle treatment that Thomas Aquinas gives to this problem is the foundation of a peculiarly Catholic understanding of the divine involvement in creation, an understanding profoundly rooted in the appearance of the God-human.

In the *Sed contra* to the first article of question 8, Thomas cites a magnificent and mysterious text from the prophet Isaiah: "Lord . . . you have accomplished all we have done" (Isa. 26:12 NABRE). Notice the beautiful tension in this line: what we indeed have done has been, nevertheless, achieved by God. We act, and God acts in us, and, in the imagination of Isaiah, there is no final contradiction between these two affirmations. This Isaian passage is a particularly clear expression of what I have called the noncompetitive relationship between God and the world. Especially in the light of the Incarnation, it becomes obvious that the proximity of God in no way overwhelms the creature but rather lifts her up to perfection and intensifies her independence and integrity. It is this paradoxical sense of the God-world relationship that Thomas Aquinas articulates in this article.

Thomas' principal argument begins with the clear assertion that God is not in created things as "part of their essence."[27] If this were the case, created reality would simply be God, and the pantheist understanding of the God-world rapport would be correct. But Thomas is no pantheist; he is not the least bit interested in collapsing God into the world in a sort of crude identification. Such a move would compromise the being of both God and the created realm, God ceasing to be God and creation ceasing to be itself. To be sure, the pantheist option is one happily embraced by us sinners, for if God is simply identified with the world of ordinary experience, we need not leave the confines of our self-complacent finitude. If God and the world are identical, then our world need never be shaken or fundamentally questioned. Thus, Aquinas must play a more subtle game.

He next rejects the possibility that God is present to the world as an "accident"—that is to say, as a qualification or attribute of finite things. If pantheism collapses God into the world, this theory renders God even less than the world. If God were an accident of finite things, he would be altogether expendable and forgettable, something that could easily be set aside. One could express this inadequate view in a more contemporary idiom by saying that God is a force of nature that influences and animates all things or that God is a dimension of psychological life. In both cases, the divine becomes an accidental or incidental accessory to the world—once more a fantasy of the self-elevating ego.

No, God is neither identified with the world nor accidental to it; rather, God is present to it as an agent:

> For an agent must be joined to that upon which it immediately acts and touch it by its power. . . . Now since God is very being by his own essence, created

---

27. *Summa theologiae* 1.8.1.

being must be his proper effect, as to ignite is the proper effect of fire. Now God causes this effect in things not only when they first begin to be but as long as they are preserved in being. . . . Therefore as long as a thing has being, God must be present to it according to its mode of being.[28]

These are among the most beautiful and remarkable words in the *Summa*, but again we must search behind the technical vocabulary to the spiritual experience that animates it. Following Aristotle, Thomas maintains that an efficient cause, an agent, must be spatially present to its effect. There must, for example, be a physical proximity between the staff that moves and the hand that moves it. But God, as we know, is efficient cause of the whole of the universe and in a remarkably exhaustive sense, since the divine reality produces not simply the motion, the change, the growth of the finite realm, but rather its very being, the very energy of its existence. Therefore, God, the agent cause of the whole, must be physically present *at all times, to all things, in the most intimate way possible.*

But being is innermost in each thing and most fundamentally inherent in all things since it is formal in respect of everything found in a thing. . . . Hence it must be that God is in all things and innermostly so [*intime*].[29]

God is not incidentally or provisionally present to the things of the world; nor is God present only to some and not to others, as some philosophies hold. No, God is in the things that he *continually makes*. As will be explored more fully in the next chapter, creation for Thomas is not a once-and-for-all event, something that took place "at the beginning of time." Rather, creation is the ongoing, continual gift of being that flows from God to the world. It is the perpetual and gracious constitution of the universe through the outflowing of the divine being. Thus, the creative agent who is God must be present to, must be in all things at the very root of their existence. Thomas is echoing in more sober language Augustine's magnificent assertion that God is *interior intimo meo* (closer to me than I am to myself), nearer to me than that which is nearest to me.[30]

As was hinted at above, this insight follows from the grounding experience of the ever-greater God in Jesus of Nazareth. As we saw in the last chapter, God enters into an unspeakably close union with Jesus without overwhelming or compromising Christ's humanity and without negating his own divinity. In light

---

28. *Summa theologiae* 1.8.1.
29. *Summa theologiae* 1.8.1.
30. Augustine, *Confessions* 3.6 (PL 32:688) (translation mine). For an English translation of this work see *Confessions*, trans. F.J. Sheed, ed. Michael P. Foley (Park Ridge, IL: Word on Fire Classics, 2017).

of the Incarnation, an entirely new paradigm for the God-world relationship has emerged: what had theretofore been seen as an opposition or rivalry could now be seen as most intimate cooperation. Is God in things? Given the event of Jesus Christ, that coming together of divine and human ecstasy, we can answer that question with Thomas' intoxicating "yes." And notice that we need not affirm this union through an awkward collapsing of God into the world or the world into God. Once more guided by the icon of Christ, we can affirm with Thomas that the universe is fully itself precisely when it is recognized as resting most intimately in the energy of God.

The play between objections and responses in this first article of question 8 is extraordinarily rich and illuminating. The first objector offers what appears to be a pious and convincing argument against God's presence in all things. The Psalmist, he reminds us, affirms that God is high above all nations—that is to say, radically transcendent to the world. But "what is above all things is not in all things."[31] On the face of it, this is a convincing counterargument to Thomas' position. Does not the intimate presence of God in and to the world compromise the otherness and strangeness of God? In celebrating God's proximity to his creation, is Thomas not stripping God of his transcendent majesty and thereby drawing him into the realm of creatures? We can hear echoes of this objection in the twentieth century in the writings of the Protestant theologian Karl Barth. Annoyed at what he took to be attempts to domesticate and control the deity, Barth cried out in favor of the *Gottheit Gottes* (the Godliness of God) and spoke of the "infinite qualitative distinction" between God and creation.[32] Indeed, nothing raised the ire of Barth more than the peculiarly Catholic (and Thomistic) doctrine of the *analogia entis* (the analogy of being), the view that there is some continuity or similarity between the infinite and the finite.[33]

In his clarification of his position in response to this criticism, Thomas implicitly unmasks a dangerous spiritual attitude.

> God is above all things by the excellence of his nature; nevertheless, he is in all things as the cause of the being of all things.[34]

What Aquinas signals here is that the dramatic, indeed infinite, difference between God and the world is a *modal* and not a spatial one. God is not transcendent

31. *Summa theologiae* 1.8.1 obj. 1.

32. Karl Barth, *The Epistle to the Romans*, trans. Edwyn Hoskyns (Oxford: Oxford University Press, 1968), 355.

33. See Karl Barth, *Church Dogmatics*, vol. 1, *The Doctrine of the Word of God*, pt. 1, trans. G.W. Bromiley (Edinburgh: T&T Clark, 1975), xii.

34. *Summa theologiae* 1.8.1 ad. 1.

to the universe inasmuch as he occupies a different "space," but inasmuch as his *way* of being is qualitatively different from that of any creature. In a word, a finite thing is a being, and God is Being itself. However, this modal otherness does not for a moment imply that God is distant or far removed from creation, quite the contrary. Precisely because he is so thoroughly other, God can be in the most intimate sense (*intime*) the ground and cause of all things. Once more a real but subtle spiritual danger is averted. In so emphasizing the difference of God, one can easily turn the divine reality into a cold and distant idol, something akin to a Greek god or a philosophical principle. The piety of Thomas' objector is thus unmasked as false and dangerous.

There is a similar dynamic at work in the conversation between the fourth objection and response. The objector maintains that the demons are beings but that God could not possibly be in such rebellious and essentially sinful spirits. Thus, it follows that God is not in all things.[35] What we witness here is a seemingly devout attempt to preserve the beauty and dignity of God by keeping him free of contact with unsavory aspects of his creation. In this view, the perfect and transcendently simple God would never lower himself to establish a relationship with a demon. Hidden in this objection is a sort of moralizing dualism that effectively accomplishes something longed for by the sinner—namely, a safe haven, a place untouched by the divine power. If God is not in the demons, then demonic behavior is something I can embrace in order to distance myself from God. If God is not in hell, then hell is somewhere I can go to get away from God.

Thomas, the master of the soul, is carefully at work in his response.

> In the demons there is their nature which is from God, and also the deformity
> of sin which is not from him; therefore, it is not to be absolutely conceded that
> God is in the demons, except with the addition, *inasmuch as they are beings*.[36]

This seems, I grant you, merely a subtle bit of medieval hairsplitting, but there is, in fact, a marvelous piece of spiritual direction here. In speaking of the demons and by extension us sinners, we must distinguish between what is true, good, and beautiful in them (their minds, their wills, their faculties, their existence) and what is evil in them (their misguided desire). Whatever pertains to being in them is good and hence grounded in the loving presence of God. In their essential structures, in their powers and in their being, they are worthwhile, beloved creatures of God and are filled up with the divine presence. What is sinful and distorted in the demons—and in us sinners—is a kind of nonbeing,

---

35. *Summa theologiae* 1.8.1 obj. 4.
36. *Summa theologiae* 1.8.1 ad. 4.

a sort of shadow or darkness, an abuse of what God has given. That sin is indeed an absence of God and hence God cannot be described as being in it. But what is interesting, especially for those of us caught in the power of sin and rebellion against God, is the extent to which God is present to us *even in our sin*. Indeed, the very capacity to reject God rests paradoxically on the energy and power of God; even in our most dramatic rebellion, we are riding the wave of God's unavoidable presence to us. And therefore *we cannot finally avoid God in and through our sin*. We cannot find refuge from the crush of the divine presence in the stance of hatred and rebellion. What this rather arcane distinction of Thomas Aquinas tells us is that we sinners can always find hope: we who flee furiously from God can never run fast enough finally to get away.

The Immutability of God

With this issue we confront one of the most contested and debated points in contemporary theology. Is it correct to say that the God of Jesus Christ, the God of passionate commitment and love, is immutable, incapable of change, indeed unresponsive? Would an insistence on this quality not undermine much of what I have been arguing throughout this book—namely, that God is properly understood only from the standpoint of the Incarnation, that fullest expression of divine compassion? And would the assertion of God's unchangeability not imply that God is a cold and self-contained principle, a Rock of Gibraltar-like monolith of being, not truly alive and vibrant? In order to respond to these legitimate questions, it is of singular importance to understand precisely what Thomas Aquinas does and does not mean by "immutability," and thus why he feels obliged to ascribe this attribute to the God of Jesus Christ.

As I have often urged, it is essential to examine the scriptural "icon" that governs and animates a Thomistic analysis. In the first article of question 9, which deals with the divine immutability, the *Sed contra* is a citation from the prophet Malachi: "I am the Lord, and I change not." What becomes clear when we examine the biblical setting is that this divine unchangeableness is tied intimately to God's covenant faithfulness. As is often the case in the prophetic literature, God is luring, cajoling his people, drawing them into deeper relationship with him. In the passage from Malachi that Aquinas cites, God is calling his people back to faithfulness and, as a sort of inspiration, he reminds them of his unchanging love. Indeed, in the very next verse, Yahweh says: "Return to me, and I will return to you" (Mal. 3:7). What becomes clear is that Thomas does not see a contradiction between God's immutability and his faithful responsiveness to his people: *au contraire*. Rather, he appreciates the unchangeableness of God as itself the condition for the possibility of God's everlasting fidelity.

In the *Respondeo* to this article, Thomas offers three arguments for the divine immutability, and I find the third the most illuminating:

> Everything which is moved acquires something by its movement, and attains to what it had not attained previously. But since God is infinite, comprehending in himself all the plenitude and perfection of all being, he cannot acquire anything new, nor extend himself to anything whereto he was not extended previously. Hence movement in no way belongs to him.[37]

It is most instructive here to note how Thomas is defining "motion." Motion is understood as the attainment or acquisition of some dimension of being previously unattained—the coming into possession of that which one lacked. It is precisely this type of motion that must be denied of God who is the supremely simple, perfect reality. The one who is the fullness of actuality cannot realize some new dimension of himself, cannot grow into a deeper or richer mode of existence, cannot "get better." Indeed, were God to move in this sense he could not possibly be that all-embracing, transcendent reality that draws the universe up out of itself in ecstasy, since God himself would be drawn by something even greater. In a word, what Thomas denies of God is the changeableness *characteristic of creatures*—that is to say, a development from nonbeing to being.

But I would argue that this denial by no means implies that other types of movement cannot be ascribed to God—namely, those changes that entail not imperfection but perfection, fullness of being. For example, the ability to enter profoundly into the thoughts and feelings of another, the capacity to respond to the needs of another—what we might term "compassion"—is not to be denied of the immutable God. Rather, as a perfection, it should be vigorously affirmed of him. Similarly, the mutability involved in a beautiful song or an elaborate dance, the changeableness of a lively and vivacious personality—such perfections are ascribable to the unchanging God of Thomas Aquinas. To return to our earlier example, the God who "cannot get any better" is utterly *unlike the Rock of Gibraltar*, which is a being at an extremely primitive level of existence. No, the perfect, unchanging God of whom Thomas speaks must be a gyroscope of energy and activity and at the same time a stable rock. He must be what Nicholas of Cusa called a *coincidentia oppositorum* (a coming together of opposites), a blending of

---

37. *Summa theologiae* 1.9.1.

qualities that seem mutually exclusive in creatures.[38] In the words of the mystical theologian Pseudo-Dionysius, God must be both great and small, both changing and unchanging, both high and low.[39] That which cannot improve must already have, in an eminent degree, all that we recognize as perfection, beauty, and truth in the created realm. Therefore, the immutable God, defended by Thomas, is no Aristotelian principle, no uncaring force, but indeed is the God disclosed in Jesus Christ as ungraspable perfection.

And once more, in making this clarification, Aquinas holds off a dangerous spiritual attitude. In claiming that God changes (in Thomas' sense of "change"), the sinner would imply that the divine reality stands in need of improvement and thus exists at the level of any finite thing. Such a being—even praised as the highest and most impressive of realities—would remain but a creature, one more finite reality striving for perfection. Were God changeable, there would be not a qualitative but merely a quantitative difference between God and the realm of creatures. And if this were the case, then God could not possibly lure creatures dramatically beyond themselves to an infinite and perfect fulfillment.

And it is precisely the sinner who wants to flee from the demands of such a call, who wishes to remain within the narrow confines of his creaturely existence and thus who finally feels compelled to affirm the changeableness of God. Once more we see the basic strategy of the rebel: turn the infinite God into something resembling a creature so as to rest comfortably in creaturely complacency. Thomas Aquinas defends the immutability of God because of the salvation he has experienced in Jesus Christ, because he has been invited by the God of Jesus to an ecstatic perfection beyond creatureliness.

The Eternity of God

In question 10, article 2, of the *Summa*, Thomas considers an attribute that most would readily ascribe to God—namely, eternity. However, in the course of the discussion, Aquinas makes some key distinctions and clarifications that help to

---

38. Nicholas of Cusa, *De docta ignorantia* 1.4, in *Nicolai de Cusa Opera Omnia*, ed. Ernestus Hoffman and Raymundus Klibansky (Hamburg: Meiner, 1932), 1:10.1–11.22. For an English translation of this work, see *Nicholas of Cusa on Learned Ignorance: A Translation and Appraisal of* De Docta Ignorantia, 2nd ed., trans. Jasper Hopkins (Minneapolis, MN: Arthur J. Banning, 1985).

39. Pseudo-Dionysius, *The Divine Names* 9.

specify what the theologian means by eternity and therefore why, precisely from a spiritual standpoint, he feels obliged to affirm this quality of God.

In the *Respondeo*, Aquinas makes the connection between immutability and eternity. Following Aristotle, he argues that time is the measure of motion or succession. "Before" and "after" are terms designating, indeed measuring, some transition or movement in nature. But God, as we have seen, is utterly beyond movement and hence cannot be measured by any temporal category.[40] For an immutable reality, there can be no "before," "during," or "after"; rather, all his being must be expressed, paradoxically, in a *nunc stans*, an eternal now.

What we notice first of all in this Thomistic analysis is that God's eternity has nothing to do with everlasting duration. It is decidedly not the case that God is a being who exists in endless time, who simply endures across centuries and aeons without passing away. It is not the case that some things last a brief time, others a long time, and God an infinitely long time. What Thomas argues is this: God is not in time at all; God is not long-lasting or short-lasting, neither fragile nor durable. Rather, the very categories of time do not apply to God because God is not one of the realities in the world whose movement or transition can be measured. We see once again the theme of the divine strangeness. If we were to picture one of the temporal beings in our experience and simply imagine it enduring for an infinite period of time, we could hold in our minds an idea of the everlasting God. But the properly eternal God, the God who cannot be captured in the categories of temporality at all, is literally unimaginable, inconceivable. Thomas here sculpts away one more creaturely quality from our conception of God in order to render the power disclosed in Jesus Christ ever more mysterious and alluring.

How is Thomas the spiritual master at work in this article? One of the greatest temptations of the sinner is to escape from God by isolating him temporally. Even under the guise of piety, one could affirm that God is a power at work "at the beginning of time." Or, in a similarly devout vein, one could say that God is the magnet luring the universe into the future. Such a sequestering of the first reality renders him effectively impotent in the here and now of one's life. When I speak in the language of mythology and say that the divine was especially active *in illo tempore* (in that time), in that sacred moment "in the beginning," I thereby distance myself from God, happily "secularizing" the time in which I live. Or, when I simply wait for God to be revealed in that marvelous eschatological "end time," I similarly sweep the divine presence from the time that concerns me now. In affirming, however paradoxically, the divine eternity, Thomas holds off these

---

40. *Summa theologiae* 1.10.2.

sinful states of mind. The God who is outside of time, over time, is *present to every moment of time*. What we call "past, present, and future" are simultaneously "present" to God and hence all "times" are sacred, touched by the divine power. Just as there is no place where one can fly to be away from God (after all, God is everywhere), so there is no time when one can be free of God. Thomas, in one more way, pushes out the contours of God, hints at the depth, breadth, and length of God, in order to cut off all sinful modes of escape.

The sinful uneasiness with the divine eternity is clearly brought out in the play between objections and responses in article 3, which considers the question of whether to be eternal belongs to God alone. The second objector formulates a clever argument in which he tries to establish a sort of rival eternity to that of God. In Jesus' parable recounted in Matthew 25, the divine judge speaks to the damned saying, "Depart you cursed into the eternal fire," thus implying that the evil eternity of hell must be affirmed alongside the eternity of God.[41] Can we hear the subtle voice of the sinner in this objection? Can we sense here the perverse desire to find freedom from the demands of God precisely in the rebellion of sin itself? Is there not here an attempt to mock the eternity of God with the equivalent eternity of hell or rejection of God? Just as in the previous question an objector denied that God could be in a demon, so here the objector argues that God's eternity cannot overwhelm and include the eternity of hell.

In response, Aquinas says,

> The fire of hell is called eternal, only because it never ends. Still, there is change in the pains of the lost. . . . Hence in hell true eternity does not exist, but rather time.[42]

Again, the distinction is made between what is authentically eternal and what is merely everlasting. In this case of rebellion against God, we are dealing with that which is, in a sense, furthest from eternity, that which is most ensconced in and conditioned by time. Indeed, one could say that one of the greatest sufferings of hell is precisely the inability to lose oneself in the timelessness of God, to be sunk, as it were, hopelessly in time. To be in hell is not to find a rival eternity; rather, it is to be cut off from the bliss of transcending time.

In the end, the affirmation of God's eternity means that we have a way out of the physical and psycho-spiritual ravages of time. To be sure, time eventually wears out our bodies, aging us, pushing us toward decline, but it also wears us out spiritually and psychologically by robbing us continually of the present

---

41. *Summa theologiae* 1.10.3 obj. 2.
42. *Summa theologiae* 1.10.3 ad. 2.

moment. Because we exist in time, we can never finally rest in the beauty of our experience. Instead, the present slips inevitably and irredeemably into the past, leaving us with only memories and impressions. To be one with the eternal God is not to intensify our sense of time (in everlastingness); on the contrary, it is to be raised up to that rapturous state of *nunc stans*, the eternal present, in which all events, all experiences, are wonderfully "now." In those rare moments that we appropriately refer to as "ecstatic," we lose a sense of time, a feeling of past, present, and future. In those moments, we and the world that surrounds us simply are.

Those ecstasies—and not, for example, the agonies of waiting endlessly in line—are proper anticipations, foretastes, of what it means to be united to the God who is eternal in Thomas' sense of the term.

The Knowledge of God

We have walked with Thomas Aquinas as he has negatively delineated and described the power that was disclosed in Jesus Christ. Not caught in any of the categories of finitude, this reality is simple, perfect, alluring, intimately present to all things, unchanging, and eternal. As such, this power draws us up beyond ourselves into a kind of ecstatic encounter. But some nagging questions remain. Is this strange and alluring reality personal? Does it or she or he *know me, love me, care about me*? To this point in the discussion we could be dealing with a still rather abstract and coldly impersonal force. Is this God that Thomas Aquinas speaks of friendly?

In question 14 of the *Summa*, Thomas begins to address these concerns by exploring various issues dealing with the knowledge of God. As we follow Thomas' discussion here it is most important to remind ourselves of a clarification made in chapter 1. When a medieval theologian speaks of knowledge, he refers not to a distant, academically respectable form of rational insight. Rather, he speaks of experience and personal participation. When Thomas wonders, therefore, whether God has knowledge, he wants to know to what extent God *experiences* himself and the world that he has made.

Let us turn now to the first article of question 14, in which our issue is explicitly raised. In the *Sed contra*, Thomas cites the magnificent passage from Paul: "O the depth of the riches of the wisdom and of the knowledge of God!" (Rom. 11:33). It is important to note the context for this citation: Paul sings of the depths of God's wisdom precisely to counter the egotistical tendency of human beings to stand above God. What immediately follows the above citation is these words: "For who has known the mind of the Lord? Or who has been his counselor?" (Rom. 11:34). The implication is that to deny knowledge of God is subtly to assert one's superiority to the divine.

The actual argument for God's knowledge in the *Respondeo* is elegant and beautiful. Thomas tells us that an intelligent being is distinguished from a nonintelligent thing by the difference in the range of their being. A rock, for example, *possesses* but one form—namely, its own: a rock is a rock. But a human being, possessed of an intelligent mind, can, through that intelligence, assume the forms of many things beyond itself. Indeed, in Thomas' phrase, the mind is *quodammodo omnia* (in a certain sense, all things); it is a sort of theater in which a full range of "forms" can appear.[43] What gives the human subject this capacity to be all things is the immateriality of the mind. Because human beings are at root spiritual or immaterial, they can reach beyond the confines of their own nature.

> Since therefore God is in the highest degree of immateriality. . . it follows that he occupies the highest place in knowledge.[44]

As spiritual in the richest possible sense, God is that reality that can enter, in a supremely affective and personal sense, into another, knowing it from within. God is able to reflect on—to possess—not only his own being but the being of all that he has created. He concerns, presses on, understands, consciously holds all possible expressions of reality. What Thomas specifies here is the precise nature of the divine presence "in" things that he spoke of earlier: God is present to all things not only ontologically but personally, knowing them, in Augustine's magnificent phrase, better than they know themselves. We notice something remarkable here: God's spirituality or immateriality does not imply God's distance from the world; on the contrary, it is precisely this quality of the divine being that enables God to be absolutely intimate and "interior" to his creation. Because God is immaterial, God can "become" one of his creatures, living in the depths of its being, luring it from within.

And is this not the divine power disclosed in Jesus Christ? The reality that ultimately concerns us and lifts us up beyond ourselves *must be a person who knows us*; if God were less than knowledgeable, we could justifiably assert our superiority to God and leave him behind. We cannot finally be "had" by a blind

---

43. *Summa theologiae* 1.14.1.
44. *Summa theologiae* 1.14.1.

cosmic force; we cannot finally be compelled by an impersonal ground of being. No, says Thomas Aquinas, the ground of being must be a person who sees me, knows me, and searches me out.

In the fifth article of this fourteenth question, Thomas most explicitly discusses the way that God knows the world, and his findings are of decisive spiritual significance. Following Aristotle, Aquinas admits that the first object of God's knowledge is God's own being: God is, as it were, intuitively and perfectly aware of himself. Then his argument continues:

> Now if anything is perfectly known, it follows of necessity that its power is perfectly known. But the power of anything can be perfectly known only by knowing to what its power extends. Since therefore the divine power extends to other things by the very fact that it is the first effective cause of all things, . . . God must necessarily know things other than himself.[45]

In short, God grasps his own reality and then understands all that he has made inasmuch as it participates in him. In reflecting on himself, God at the same time reflects upon all that he continually touches with his presence. For Thomas, God sees the universe *in and through himself*, through the prism of the divine being. What is wonderful here is the spiritual truth: God sees things properly, in their deepest identity, in their rootedness in the divine. God appreciates the universe not as a separate and independent realm of reality but precisely as an outpouring from his own love. One of the ways that we could describe the fallen mind—the mind characterized by sin—is a tendency to lose this vision of the world, to see the universe outside of its divine aura and separate from its divine ground. It is, for instance, a mind marked by an excessive empiricism and materialism that stubbornly misses the deepest truth about the created realm, that arrogantly brackets the spiritual dimension as something unworthy of serious attention. Or it is a mind exclusively attuned to the movements and affairs of the finite that cannot see the infinite lurking everywhere or cannot appreciate the divine soil out of which all created existence grows. To know the world properly, Thomas implies, is to see it with the eyes of God—that is to say, to see it only through the "veil" of God's being.

The play between the second objection to this article and its response is most interesting inasmuch as it displays once more the false piety of the sinner. In line with classical epistemology, the objector argues that the object known is the perfection of the knower. Thus, if God knows something other than himself—namely, the world—then that object will bring God to greater

---

45. *Summa theologiae* 1.14.5.

perfection and will be, in some sense, nobler than God.[46] As is usually the case with Thomas' objections, there is great common sense here. Whatever I know in some way stands outside of me, presses itself upon me, and brings my mind to reverence and obedience. To know something is, in a word, to acknowledge one's indebtedness to that thing. But this seems to be impossible to the perfect and self-sufficient God, and hence God cannot know the world. Piously defending the independence and perfection of God, the objector effectively drives God out of the world of created things. And once more the fantasy of the sinful ego is realized: a universe free of a prying, knowing God who sees our actions and peers deeply into our minds and hearts.

In response, Aquinas then highlights the priority of images in the divine mind. The image of a stone, for instance, perfects the created mind by bringing it to greater actuality, but, says Thomas, the images of created things are in the divine mind "before" the created things themselves, acting indeed as their archetypes.[47] Thus, God's knowledge of the world does not perfect God; it does not bring to God something God did not already have. Rather, God's knowledge is what perfects the *world*. This last point is central: God does not stand outside of the world, deriving knowledge from it; on the contrary, the world derives its being from the knowledge of it that God continually pours into it. God does not know the world because the world exists; the world exists because God knows it.

We notice again the subtle spiritual direction at work here. No creature must ever think that God's mind is dependent upon him; no finite reality should ever see itself as in a position to manipulate God. Rather, all creatures are dependent upon, and beholden to, the divine knowing by which they exist. Once more we are being urged to humble ourselves before the ever-greater power disclosed in Christ. More specifically, we are encouraged to become a sheer transparence to the divine knowing that flows through us.

This clarification is especially helpful given the terrible consequences that follow from the dominance of the mind. The mind is one of the most powerful weapons in the arsenal of the self-elevating ego. The mind is frequently used by the sinner as an aggressive tool to dominate, take apart, analyze, and finally manipulate the world in which he moves: all must come into the purview of the controlling intelligence. And, unfortunately, God does not escape the grasp of the manipulative mind. God becomes all too frequently one more object for the sinful ego to master and "know." In his discussion of the knowledge of God, Thomas Aquinas consistently challenges this pretension of the domineering

---

46. *Summa theologiae* 1.14.5 obj. 2.
47. *Summa theologiae* 1.14.5 ad. 2.

intelligence. We are in proper relationship with God when we see ourselves and our world as God sees them—or better, when we allow ourselves to be known by the infinite power that continually creates us. Once more, the God of Jesus Christ invites the reversal that is ecstasy.

The Will and Love of God

In affirming intelligence of God, Thomas Aquinas fundamentally proves that the first and perfect reality is a person, a "someone" possessed of consciousness. But is this person simply an abstract and distant knower, or is he characterized by concern and by love? In some ways, this is the most elemental and gripping theological question: Does the ground of being, the source of all that is, give himself to me in love? And do I therefore finally have the courage to be? Is there ultimately a loving foundation for my life despite all of its pain and setbacks and disappointments? Does God's will reach out to me in providential concern? These questions are broached in question 19 of the *Summa theologiae*.

In the first article of question 19, Aquinas shows that God's will follows necessarily from his intellect. When an intelligent nature understands the good as good, it automatically either pursues it or rests in it. And both pursuing and enjoying are acts of the will. Now, inasmuch as God understands himself as good, he necessarily rests or rejoices in the good that he assuredly is, and this divine joyfulness is identical to the divine will.

> And so there must be will in God, since there is intellect in him. And as his intellect is his own existence, so is his will.[48]

Thomas implies here that God's being is characterized by celebration and joy. To be God is to rest in, to savor, the good. In language that should be familiar to us by now, the divine being, marked by will, is nothing but ecstasy, a constant act of finding pleasure in the good possessed. What does God do then? A completely valid and theologically accurate response would be that God enjoys himself, loving and delighting in what he has.[49]

Once it is affirmed in no uncertain terms the satisfaction that God finds in resting in the perfection of his own being, it becomes rather difficult to understand why God would ever will anything outside of himself. We saw in the

---

48. *Summa theologiae* 1.19.1.
49. *Summa theologiae* 1.19.1 ad. 2.

last question dealing with the divine intellect that God *knows* all those things that share in his being; but does he *will* them, could he possibly care about them, lost as he is in the wonder of his own reality? Wouldn't the God of infinite self-satisfaction be, necessarily, narcissistic? Obviously, such divine narcissism would be, once more, the fantasy of the rebellious ego: a God so wrapped up in himself that he is utterly indifferent to the being and activity of his creation. Thomas' analysis of God's capacity to will what is other is his attempt to correct this sickness of the soul.

Thomas' argument is one of the clearest and most passionate presentations of the divine ecstasy that can be found in his work:

> For natural things have a natural inclination not only toward their own proper good, to acquire it if not possessed, and, if possessed, to rest therein; but also to spread abroad their own good amongst others, so far as possible. . . . It pertains, therefore, to the nature of the will to communicate as far as possible to others the good possessed; and especially does this pertain to the divine will, from which all perfection is derived in some kind of likeness.[50]

God cannot contain himself. Just as someone who is in a festive mood cannot help but bubble over in love and good cheer, so God cannot hold himself in, cannot refrain from sharing his good feeling with another. In one sense, Thomas implies here that God cannot finally rest in the goodness that he possesses; rather, his joyful will jumps about, spills over, overflows. God wills others in order to allow them to share in the ecstasy that he has.

Thus, the grounding and sustaining source of all that is, the perfect and unchanging one, is a person endowed with mind and will and therefore someone who cajoles and draws the created universe to himself. Thomas gives greatest specification to this idea in question 20 of the *Summa*, where he speaks of the love of God. If, as we have argued, Aquinas' work is indeed a reflection upon the revelation of God in Jesus Christ, then this *quaestio* represents a sort of climax of the theological enterprise, for here we come to the description of God that is central to the New Testament witness. What appears in the life, death, and Resurrection of Christ is, for St. John the Evangelist, the stunning fact that God is *love*. Let us follow St. Thomas Aquinas as he attempts to articulate the same insight.

In the first article of question 20, Thomas spells out the nature of love as the "first movement of the will."[51] Love is the will's basic affection for the good,

---

50. *Summa theologiae* 1.19.2.
51. *Summa theologiae* 1.20.1.

whether possessed or not. When someone has the good, he loves it as something he delights in, and when someone lacks the good, he loves it as something he hopes for. In either case, love is the elemental and grounding force, the deepest "personality" and energy of the will. Even when the will turns against an evil, it does so out of more primordial love for some other good.

> Hence in whomsoever there is will and appetite, there must also be love, since if the first is wanting, all that follows is also wanting. Now it has been shown that will is in God, and hence we must attribute love to him.[52]

God is fundamentally a passion, an energy, an activity. Once more we can see that Thomas' insistence on God's immutability and perfection in no way involves a denial of God's liveliness. It is none other than the perfectly realized ground of all there is who is a great wave of love.

Now, it should be clear that in making this claim Thomas' spiritual direction is eminently at work. It is obviously the sinner, resistant to the lure and attraction of God, who would happily imagine that God is devoid of love. Were God not loving, the sinner could go about her business in self-absorption and self-elevation without fear of divine intervention or interference. However, a God who is love, we all realize in the depths of our hearts, is a God *who will not leave us alone* in our sin, a God who will bother us and prompt us and push us to transformation. Not only is God endowed with the personalizing qualities of intellect and will; God is, above all, possessed of a driving passion toward the world that he has made, especially toward those rational creatures whom he wants to elevate to a share in his own life. This love appears wondrous to those on the path of life and fearsome to those who are clinging to themselves in rebellion against God. Thomas, the master of the soul, stubbornly preaches this beautiful and harsh truth about the God who will not let go of us. And again, where does he derive this insight finally but from the experience of unsurpassable love that was disclosed to him in Jesus Christ: there is nothing greater than that God becomes human; there is no love more profound than this gift of divine condescension.

In the exchange between the first objection and response in this article, Thomas makes an important clarification with regard to the nature of the divine love, which holds off a very subtle ruse of the sinful soul. The objector argues that since love is a passion and since there are no passions in the immutable God, it follows that God cannot be characterized by love.[53] Clinging to the

---

52. *Summa theologiae* 1.20.1.
53. *Summa theologiae* 1.20.1 obj. 1.

unchangeability of the divine, the objector wants to turn God into someone distant and indifferent, too cold to be possessed of a passion as "warm" as love. Thomas' answer is illuminating. In us, who are composed of mind and body, the movements of the spirit are always accompanied by corresponding passions in the body: moods, emotions, feelings, etc. But God is not a composition of spirit and matter and hence in God there can exist powerful urges and movements of the will—attraction, desire, compassion, love—which do not entail the corresponding bodily movements that we generally refer to as passions.[54]

This clarification is of great contemporary relevance. On the one hand, Thomas corrects the objector's assertion that God's incorporeality precludes God's love for the world, and, on the other hand, he anticipates the danger of identifying the divine love with passion in the ordinary sense of the term. It would indeed be a fantasy of the sinful ego to identify God's love with a sort of feeling or passion of the body, since, by their very nature, passions are fleeting, unreliable, and manipulable. Were the divine love something analogous to a bodily passion, it would come and go, fluctuating according to mood and whim. And it would also be subject to enormous manipulation and control on the part of the sinner. We all know from direct experience how our passions can be skillfully and sometimes painfully manipulated by another: they can be turned off or turned on, intensified or relaxed, heated up or cooled down all by the words and behavior of those around us. Were God's love like an emotion, the sinner could toy with it, now awakening it, now dampening it, now delighting it, now frustrating it.

In this exchange, Thomas Aquinas insists that the divine love that comes to us in Christ Jesus, which is identical to the divine being itself, which creates and holds up the universe, is nothing as insubstantial, fleeting, and unpredictable as a bodily passion or emotion. Rather, it is the rock upon which the world is based and the sure foundation upon which sinners can confidently rebuild their lives. At the same time, this non-emotional love is not the least bit cold. As we have seen, it is the heart and soul of God, the great act by which God goes out of himself in ecstasy to share his joy with his creatures. By walking this middle ground and making some key linguistic clarifications, Aquinas guides the sinner into right relationship with the divine love.

---

54. *Summa theologiae* 1.20.1 ad. 1.

Conclusion

The psychologist C.G. Jung once remarked that he had dipped into the writings of St. Thomas Aquinas and found the experience rather unrewarding.[55] Undoubtedly Jung, like many others, encountered what appeared to be a terribly dry rationalism in the well-ordered texts of the *Summa theologiae*, an attempt to capture the elusive spirit of the divine in arguments and distinctions and syllogisms. What I have tried to show, in this chapter especially, is that the spirit of Jesus Christ, the spirit of the ever-greater and ungraspable God, blows through the dusty pages of Thomas Aquinas' works. Thomas is decidedly *not trying to capture or define the divine*; on the contrary, he is attempting to show us precisely how to *avoid the temptation of such definition*. He is demonstrating how the soul can be liberated in the act of surrendering to the God who reveals himself as an unsurpassable and ecstatic power in Jesus Christ.

Thus, the *simple* God is the God who cannot be understood or controlled; the *good* God is the one who captivates us and draws us out of ourselves; the *God who is present to the world* is the divine power that will not leave us alone, that insinuates itself into our blood and bones; the *eternal* God is the one who invites us into the ecstasy of being beyond time; the *immutable* God is the rock upon which we can build our lives; the God of *knowledge and love* is the spirit who searches us and knows us, who seeks us and who will never abandon us.

It is this all-embracing, all-captivating, all-entrancing, all-surrounding power that Thomas Aquinas seeks to celebrate.

---

55. In a letter to Victor White, Jung expressed dissatisfaction with Aquinas' treatment of the problem of evil: "I also took a dive into S. Thomas, but I did not feel refreshed afterwards" (*The Jung–White Letters*, ed. Ann Conrad Lammers and Adrian Cunningham [London: Routledge, 2007], 141).

Chapter Three

CREATION: THE NOTHING
THAT IS EVERYTHING

Meister Eckhart, the fourteenth-century Rhineland mystic, argued that all things in the universe exist in God. So intimate is this connectedness between the divine and the creaturely that the best way to reach God, he says, is to sink into him, to find him at the root and core of one's own being. So complete is the dependency of the creature upon the divine power in which he swims, that the creature is not so much a thing as a *relationship*. The mystical "breaking-through" of which Meister Eckhart speaks is not a leaping out of this world to a contact with a supernatural supreme being, but is rather none other than an awareness of one's own divine root and heritage, one's inescapable participation in the divine fire.[1] Now, some of this language strikes us as questionable, vaguely pantheistic, even heretical. However, we recall from the introduction that Meister Eckhart was a Dominican brother of Thomas Aquinas, indeed one of Thomas' successors in the chair of theology at the University of Paris. It is my conviction that in his mystical writings Eckhart simply draws out the implications of Friar Thomas' doctrine of creation. To be sure, Eckhart does so in language that is far more poetic and evocative than Thomas', but the ideas that animate Eckhart's sermons and mystical writings come, remarkably often, from the seemingly arid metaphysics of Aquinas.

It is so easy to miss the spiritual power in the doctrine of creation. We all rather naturally accept the fact that God, at the beginning of time, brought forth the universe of finite things that now exists in separation from him. For most of us such a view is innocuous enough and calls for no great spiritual transformation on our part. What I hope to show in this chapter is that such an understanding is altogether alien to the thought of St. Thomas Aquinas. For Aquinas, the doctrine of creation is of decisive spiritual power inasmuch as it calls the believer to an

---

1. "German Sermon 52," in *Meister Eckhart: The Essential Sermons, Commentaries, Treatises, and Defense*, trans. Edmund Colledge and Bernard McGinn (Mahwah, NJ: Paulist, 1981), 203.

act of radical self-emptying and to an acknowledgment that one finds oneself precisely in total dependency.

As we have come to expect, Thomas interprets creation—the fundamental rapport between God and the world—in light of the experience of Jesus Christ. This means, basically, that the world—in all of its particularity and peculiarity, in each of its nooks and crannies—is filled, every moment and in the most intimate way possible, with the sustaining presence of God. The universe is constantly held up by, and suffused with, the creating power of the ground of being. At every instant, God brings the world from nonbeing into being, illumining it as the sun illumines the sky. This divine "shining" is creation, and allowing oneself to be "shone through" is to be a creature.

And all of this implies that the doctrine of creation is a complex and vitally important instance of spiritual direction. In articulating the nature of creation, Thomas Aquinas, I will argue, does much more than make some metaphysical clarifications. Instead, he attempts to move his reader into a stance of sheer receptivity and total openness vis-à-vis the gift of being that pours continually forth from the divine source. In the course of this chapter, we will follow Thomas' analysis of creation as it is found in two major texts, the *Summa theologiae* and the disputed question *De potentia Dei* (on the power of God). Through an examination of his texts dealing with the creative power of God, the bringing forth of the world *ex nihilo* (from nothing), and continual creation, I will try to show that Thomas Aquinas is the great theological inspiration for a healthy "creation" spirituality.

The Power of God

In order to speak of creation at all, we must first address the problem of the divine power—that is to say, God's capacity to produce something outside of himself. We saw in the previous chapter that God, precisely as characterized by love, is "diffusive of himself." He tends to overflow in an ecstatic sharing of his existence. But how and under what conditions does this self-offering take place and what are its limits? It is to these questions that Thomas turns in his examination of the power of God.

In the first article of the opening question of the *De potentia*, Thomas wonders whether it is correct to say that God has power.[2] In the *Sed contra*, Aquinas

2. Thomas Aquinas, *Disputed Questions on the Power of God* (hereafter, *The Power of God*) 1.1.

cites the mysterious saying of Jesus in Matthew's Gospel: "God is able from these stones to raise up children to Abraham" (Matt. 3:9). This quotation indicates something that we must never forget in this exploration of Thomas' understanding of creation—namely, the intimate link between God's power and the act of salvation. Never an arbitrary expression of might, the divine *potentia* is exercised for the sake of raising up children to Abraham, for the sake of inviting the world into communion with its Creator. We recall that when speaking of the Incarnation, Thomas argued that God's power is fully revealed in Christ because there is nothing greater than that God becomes human. This means that the might of God is no more blazingly evident than in the act of self-forgetting love in which God joined his creation in order to raise it up again.

In the *Respondeo*, Aquinas affirms that God's *potentia* (power) is absolute and unlimited precisely because God, as simple, is the fullness of reality. Since there is no restriction to the divine existence, there is no action that God cannot perform; there is no limit to the divine expressiveness and outreach. From a spiritual standpoint, this assertion of God's power is obviously of great moment. Wherever the sinner finds himself, he is within the "range" of God's press, God's touch. There is, as we have seen in other contexts, no neutral ground upon which a creature could stand in opposition to God. Indeed, God's power holds us up, surrounds us, envelops us—whether we like it or not.

However, in the ensuing articles, Thomas poses several rather interesting questions concerning what seems to be God's inability to do certain things. For example, in article 3, Thomas wonders whether God can do those things that are impossible to nature?[3] The biblical citation in the *Sed contra* is once more quite striking: "With God nothing is impossible" (Luke 1:37). These are, of course, the words of the angel to Mary at the time of the Annunciation, assuring her that what seems impossible to her is in fact possible to God. What this passage reveals, according to Thomas, is that God's power can accomplish more in us than we ever dreamed possible, that God can break through the barriers of our complacency and cynicism and bring forth life where we thought only death could reign. What the angel discloses to all believers is that we ought never to set limits to the expressiveness of God's graciousness and the wonderful, playful surprise of God's intervention. In this sense, God can do what seems "impossible," unthinkable, unimaginable according to the natural assumptions of the mind.

For a more recent translation of *De potentia Dei* that modifies the disputed question format to improve readability, see Thomas Aquinas, *The Power of God*, trans. Richard J. Regan (Oxford: Oxford University Press, 2012).

3. Thomas Aquinas, *The Power of God* 1.3.

However, as he explains in the *Respondeo* to this article, there are certain things that are impossible to natural agents and even to God: those that involve a logical contradiction or some undermining of the structures of being.

> His action cannot terminate otherwise than principally in being and secondarily in nonbeing. Consequently he cannot make yes and no to be true at the same time, nor any of those things which involve such an impossibility. Nor is he said to be unable to do these things through lack of power, but through a lack of possibility, such things being intrinsically impossible.[4]

What Thomas means here really is quite simple: God can do everything. What he cannot do is produce nonbeing; what he cannot bring about is what cannot possibly exist. He cannot, in a word, make what is not a thing. Hence, as Thomas indicates, God cannot square a circle or make 2+2 equal anything but 4, precisely because such eventualities cannot be. These clarifications are, once more, of enormous spiritual importance. God is not a supreme being squatting outside the world and arbitrarily "playing" with it, undermining it, turning it upside down. The French philosopher René Descartes imagined that God in his sovereign greatness could change the laws of mathematics or even the laws of morality if he so desired. For Descartes, 2+2=4 only because God arbitrarily decided that it should be; and adultery is morally objectionable only because God determined as much.[5] If the fancy caught him, God could deign that those laws be reversed.

Thomas Aquinas couldn't be in stronger disagreement with this voluntarism of Descartes. For Thomas, God is not a distant supreme being existing outside the world, but rather the act of Being itself, the creative ground of the universe. Hence, to undermine the basic structures of nature is to undermine himself; to contradict the world is to contradict himself. For Aquinas, an arbitrary Cartesian God would be a source not of comfort but of unbearable anxiety: How would I ever be able to root my life if the ground could shift fundamentally at any moment? How could I find ultimate security if God himself were capable of changing on a whim? For Thomas Aquinas, the God of covenant fidelity, the God of unchanging love, is this firm ground of existence *that cannot be untrue to himself or to what he has made.* God's power is, as St. Anselm has it, the capacity, not to say yes or no, but rather the capacity to say only yes. Once more we see that the sinner *can rest comfortably* in the divine presence and power, finding in

---

4. *The Power of God* 1.3.

5. See, for instance, René Descartes, "First Letter to Mersenne" and "Second Letter to Mersenne," in *The Philosophical Writings of Descartes*, vol. 3, *The Correspondence*, trans. John Cottingham et al. (Cambridge: Cambridge University Press, 1991), 23–24.

it an unshakeable support. The God who "cannot" do the impossible is like a parent who "could not" turn on her own children.

When he was in the trenches during the First World War, watching his friends die and feeling the concussions of the exploding shells, young Paul Tillich would read from the letter to the Romans: "For I am convinced that neither death, nor life, nor angels, nor rulers, nor things present, nor things to come, nor powers, nor height, nor depth, nor anything else in all creation, will be able to separate us from the love of God in Christ Jesus our Lord" (Rom. 8:38–39).[6] This assurance of God's unbreakable faithfulness would give him and his colleagues hope. Thomas finds the same hope in speaking of a God who cannot be untrue to himself or to what he has made through his power.

Creation from Nothing

Having shown that God has power that is infinite in its outreach, salvific in its intent, and faithful to itself, Thomas next turns to the central question: whether God can create something from nothing.[7] It is terribly important to understand the revolutionary quality of this question. Many myths and legends and philosophies speak of a God who forms or fashions some preexisting "stuff" into the universe as we know it. God makes the world out of either his own substance or out of earth, air, fire, or unformed matter. In this case, the Creator is like a potter or an artisan, fashioning the universe "out of something." What Thomas is wondering in his famous question is whether God truly creates—that is to say, makes the universe *ex nihilo*, out of nothing, drawing it neither from his own being or from anything else but simply from nonbeing into being.

Thomas seeks to answer this question by referring to what we saw in the previous chapter to be the prime divine "attribute"—namely, simplicity. God is not any type of being but rather the act of Being itself. God does not exist in this way or that; God simply is. This means, of course, that if God decides to make something other than himself, he must be responsible for the *entirety of that thing's being*, and not only for some aspect thereof. If God is the fullness of reality, then whatever exists other than God must derive the totality of its being

---

6. See Wilhelm and Marion Pauck, *Paul Tillich: His Life and Thought* (New York: Harper & Row, 1976), 1:49.

7. Thomas Aquinas, *The Power of God* 3.1.

from God and from no other source. Thus, there is no stuff from which or out of which God makes the world:

> By his action, he produces the whole subsistent being, without anything having existed before (since he is the source of all being). . . . For this reason, he can make a thing from nothing, and this action of his is called creation.[8]

What is the spiritual import of this teaching? First, since God truly *creates,* there is absolutely no aspect of finite reality that does not flow from the divine source. There is nothing in the world, in nature, in the cosmos, or in us, that is not, in every detail, the result of God's creative act. There is, consequently, nothing that is finally "secular" or "profane"; instead, everything is, in principle, at the root of its being, sacred. The great counterposition here would be that of the Gnostics who claim that God touches and is responsible for the spiritual realm while remaining opposed to the evil of the material dimension. In affirming creation from nothing, Thomas shows his radical disagreement with this sort of dualism. For him, as for the author of Genesis, all being is redolent of the divine and hence worthy of reverence and celebration: all ground is holy ground, all places are holy places, all times are sacred times.

Pierre Teilhard de Chardin maintained in a well-known aphorism that "nothing here below is profane for those who know how to see."[9] In Teilhard's theory, the entire cosmos is, from the beginning, touched and suffused with the divine energy, a power that pushes it, shapes it, and finally draws it to its fulfillment.[10] The fire of God, he says, is the inescapable beginning, middle, and end of the evolutionary process. It is the divine spirit that compels primitive life forms to evolve in the direction of greater complexity and interiority until they reach the level of conscious awareness. And it is the same spirit that pushes the human heart upward and outward toward union with God. Everywhere, and at all times, and in every corner of the universe, God's creative power is at work. Teilhard felt that the problem with the believers of his time (and I would argue of our time as well) is that they don't know how to *see* this divine omnipresence. As a result, they divide the real into two sharply separated realms: the sacred and the secular, the supernatural and the natural, the holy and the profane. And thus they feel, in their very immersion in the world and its values, an alienation from

---

8. *The Power of God* 3.1.

9. Pierre Teilhard de Chardin, *The Divine Milieu,* ed. and trans. Bernard Wall (New York: Harper Perennial, 2001), 30.

10. For a collection of works that explore his theological evolutionary vision, see Pierre Teilhard de Chardin, *Writings in Time of War,* trans. René Hague (London: Collins, 1968). For his most mature articulation of his evolutionary cosmology, see Pierre Teilhard de Chardin, *The Phenomenon of Man,* trans. Bernard Wall (New York: Harper Perennial, 1959).

God, a sense of God's distance and absence. The point of the spiritual life for Teilhard is to wake up, to open our eyes, to learn once more how to see.

Teilhard's reflections represent a contemporary and more "scientific" version of Thomas' teaching on creation *ex nihilo* (from nothing). If God is responsible for every nook and cranny of the cosmos, then all things are burning with the divine fire, all things begin, endure, and reach their completion in God. Like Teilhard, Thomas is teaching the believer how to *see* this all-encompassing divine presence.

It is interesting to note that Teilhard de Chardin was only one of several theologians in the first half of the twentieth century who, in various ways, expressed uneasiness with the inherited understanding of the relationship between nature and grace. In the formal theology of pre-Vatican II Catholicism, there was, many of these theologians felt, an exaggerated emphasis on the distinction between the "divine" and the "created," so much so that the natural realm was seen as basically self-sufficient, with its own goals and integrity.[11]

But this meant that "ordinary" experience remains fundamentally untouched by grace. As we saw in chapter 1, this sharp dichotomy couldn't be further from the mind of Thomas Aquinas. From the beginning and at its deepest roots, human experience is open to graced transformation. The human heart is hunger and thirst for God, and God is that power that lifts us up and remakes us. In light of the Incarnation, we see that God moves comfortably within the confines of nature, mixing with it and inviting it to transformation. Perhaps most profoundly, in this teaching on creation *ex nihilo*, it becomes clear that literally nothing stands between the world and its divine source. There is thus no sharp delineation between the sacred and the secular, but rather all of "secularity" shines with the light of the sacred. All of the ordinary is filled with extraordinary grace.

This properly Thomistic view is not far from Paul Tillich's understanding of the God-world relationship. Since God, for Tillich, is the ground of being itself, God is found at the heart of nature and at the heart of culture. The "world" and "secular society" are not obstacles to an experience of God; on the contrary, they are sacraments of the divine presence, bearers of God's reality and life.[12] God is

11. For a classic expression of this critique, see Henri de Lubac, *The Mystery of the Supernatural*, trans. Rosemary Sheed (New York: Herder & Herder, 1967).

12. See, for instance, Paul Tillich, *Theology of Culture*, ed. Robert C. Kimball (Oxford: Oxford University Press, 1959), 41: "The universe is God's sanctuary. Every work day is a day of the Lord, every supper a Lord's supper, every work the fulfillment of a divine task, every joy a joy in God. In all preliminary concerns, ultimate concern is present, consecrating them. Essentially the religious and the secular are not separated realms. Rather they are within each other."

found in the hushed forests, in the cry of the hawk, in the roiled ocean—and God is found in the machinations of the lawyer searching for justice, in the soaring tone of the opera singer's voice, and in the serious playfulness of a game of baseball. We don't rise above these various events and activities to find their divine source; rather, as Eckhart pointed out, we sink into them toward their divine ground. It is my contention that we can make these observations only in light of the strange and remarkable doctrine of creation from nothing.

Creation as a Relationship

As Thomas' analysis of creation unfolds, we witness a sort of revolution in our understanding of ourselves in relation to God. If what Thomas says is true, then we are fundamentally different than we had imagined; if this understanding is correct, then we have been living under the influence of an illusion. Like a patient Zen master, Thomas, the spiritual director, is trying to move us out of the realm of illusion and misperception. But what is this mistaken view? How have we misconstrued ourselves in our rapport with God? Thomas' basic answer is this: we have forgotten that God is the one who creates us from nothing, and hence we have tended to see ourselves as *beings set apart from God, things that have a relationship with God.* What Aquinas wants us to appreciate is that, as creatures, we *are a relationship to the divine power.* He wants us to see that we live and move and have our being in the very energy of God (cf. Acts 17:28). The tragedy of sin, from a Thomistic standpoint, is that we attempt to find ourselves by affirming our difference from God. At the heart of the creation teaching is what I call the metaphysics of the Gospel: the more we lose ourselves in God, the more we find our authentic selves, and the more we cling to our independence of the divine, the more we lose our souls.

Thomas explores this theme in article 3 of question 3 of the *De potentia*. He wonders "whether creation is something really in the creature." More precisely, he wants to know the "locale" and the "nature" of the creative act whereby a finite thing comes into being: Is it "in" the creature or "in between" God and the creature or, perhaps, only at the moment when a particular thing comes to be? In light of what we have seen so far, it should first of all be clear that creation is not a change of some sort, not a transition from one state to another. For what changes already exists in some way and simply receives through the change some new *way of existing.* But creation is *from nothing* and hence there is no already-existing something out there that receives or accepts it. To be created is not, therefore, to take on a new way of being; rather, it is to come to be in the full sense of the term. Thus, creation is not "between" the Creator and the creature, not simply the vague influence of the former on the latter.

Once more, this cosmological clarification has personal and spiritual implications. It is the fantasy of the sinner that creation is merely a change, for such a view assumes that the creature has only an extrinsic relation to God. If God only moves or affects me, then I can find my substantial independence of God. If I relate to God primarily as to a mover, then I can find refuge from the press of God in the secret recesses of my own being, that part of me that is untouched by the divine:

> Therefore, creation does not denote an approach to being, nor a change effected by the Creator, but merely a beginning of existence, and a relation to the Creator from whom the creature receives its being. Consequently, creation is really nothing but a relation of the creature to the Creator together with a beginning of existence.[13]

This is one of the most marvelous and uplifting passages in the writings of Thomas Aquinas if we can but probe beneath its scholastic surface. Creation is the breath of God breathed out in such a way as to constitute the whole reality of the world and all things in it. It is the beginning of the world not in a chronological sense but in a spiritual sense: God is the root and ground, the profoundest source of all being. Gerard Manley Hopkins, the Jesuit poet, says in one of his best-known poems that "there lives the dearest freshness deep down things."[14] This, it seems to me, is what Thomas Aquinas means by the act of creation. Despite the suffering that we face on a daily basis, despite the gloomy prospects of global politics, despite our fear of the unknown future, "there lives the dearest freshness deep down," there exists a source of life and hope and love that is the divine power. And this power can never be exhausted because it is the very being of the creature, it is the presence of God's love in us. Thus, the more we call upon it, the more we give it away, the more we draw from it, the more abundant it becomes.

And, once more, if creation is the act by which the whole of one's being is constituted, then the creature is *nothing but a relationship* to God. In light of Thomas' understanding of creation, relation, not substance, is the primary

---

13. Thomas Aquinas, *The Power of God* 3.3.

14. Gerard Manley Hopkins, "God's Grandeur," in *Ignatian Collection*, ed. Holly Ordway and Daniel Seseske (Park Ridge, IL: Word on Fire Classics, 2020), 179.

category of reality. It is not as though God makes *things* with which he then establishes a relationship; on the contrary, from the beginning, all "things" *already* are relations to the divine source. We are most ourselves precisely when we acknowledge that what we are, most fundamentally, is a rapport, a play, a dynamic relation to God.

Thus, creation is *quaedam relatio* (a certain relation) to God *cum novitate essendi* (with the newness of being). This last phrase is marvelous. When we realize what it means to be a creature, we know that we are never far from renewal, from freshness of life, from endless possibility. We are, after all, nothing but this ongoing outpouring from the divine love and hence there is always "a spring of water gushing up to eternal life" in us (John 4:14). The key to Thomas' creation spirituality is to enter ever more intimately and profoundly into this mystery of who we are: at the root of ourselves, there is nothing but *novitas essendi*, newness of being. Again, it is my contention that this understanding of creation comes not from Aristotle's philosophy (indeed it contradicts Aristotle), but rather from the stunning event of Jesus Christ. What did Thomas see in Christ? We recall from the first chapter that for him Jesus was a sheer transparency to the Father, an *instrumentum* (an instrument) completely responsive to the divine will. In Jesus, God's power is perfectly able to flow because of the concordance in him between the divine and the human. In this sense, it is Christ himself who reveals what it means fully to be a creature. Christ is the one in whom the "freshness of being" was continually apparent, endlessly available. We recall from chapter 1 that for Thomas the humanity of Jesus was like a fountain filled to overflowing with the grace of God. And we also recall that in his humanity Jesus is one with us. Therefore, in his human nature, in his sheer obedience to the will of the divine, he is the model of what the created world should look like in relation to God: in a word, Christ is the "nothing" that becomes a conduit for the "everything" that is God. As such, he discloses the nature of the relationship that is the creature.

Now, what does it mean to emphasize the relationality of the creature as much as Thomas has? It means, as I hinted above, that we must rid ourselves of the illusion that we are separate, self-contained "things" existing in a world of other things. It is much closer to the truth to say that we are processes, unfoldings, "flows of energy." And thus the more we surrender to God in self-forgetting love, the more we find ourselves and the more we see with real metaphysical clarity who we are. When we cling to our independence, our separateness, we live stubbornly in a realm of illusion and thus, on a psychological and spiritual level, we fall into sadness and alienation.

In a word, it is only in *ecstasy* that we come fully to ourselves. The radical gift of self that Thomas Aquinas sees in the Incarnation—God surrendering himself out of love and Jesus offering himself in response—*becomes the model for understanding the nature of creation*. The more the world resembles the ecstatic nature of God and the more it mimics the transparency of Christ to the divine power, the more it finds itself. Thomas is no defender of pantheism; neither does he advocate some sort of absorption of the creature into God. Rather, inspired by the stunning poetry of Christian theology, he speaks of a creation that is most itself when it clings least to its independence. He sings of a finite realm that finds itself precisely in the self-abandonment of love. Once more, it is the icon of the Incarnation—divine and human ecstasy—that informs Thomas' vision.

And this is why we are commanded to "love the Lord your God with all your heart, and with all your soul, and with all your mind" (Matt. 22:37). This is not a merely ethical commandment, a recommendation for fostering the good life; it is a matter of life and death, of illusion or reality. The more we love God and let go of our awful seriousness and defensiveness, the more we discover correctly who we are. Christ's command to love God does not simply urge us to adopt a new type of behavior; rather, it opens a window to the soul. What Thomas implicitly defends here is what contemporary theologians call "panentheism," the existence of all things in God.

And is it not the case that so much of the struggle of human life flows from this failure to see properly who we are? Why do we engage in violence? Why are we crippled by hatred and envy? Why do we fall so often into a life-denying self-absorption? Because, I would argue, we don't appreciate our creatureliness. When I realize that I am nothing but an outflow of the divine love, nothing but an ongoing gift, I realize that there is no "self" that requires defense. I am not one being among many fighting for primacy; on the contrary, I am a sheer dependency upon the divine grace. And thus my life need not be an awful struggle for dominance, a continual warfare against God, against nature, against my fellows, all those who threaten my "turf." The doctrine of creation, as articulated by Thomas Aquinas, enables me to let go, to relax, to find myself in losing myself.

Furthermore, as Meister Eckhart pointed out so clearly, Thomas' understanding of creation as relation means that all things in the universe, especially my fellow human beings, are related one to the other. All reality—from the simplest element to the farthest star, from a microbe to an archangel—flows, here and now, from the same source and exists in the same dependency. At the center, all things are family, in the most dramatic sense possible, siblings to one another. Before Thomas put it in more theoretical language, Francis of Assisi sang the same idea when he raised his voice to "Brother Sun" and "Sister Moon," to "Brother Fire" and "Sister Bodily Death."[15]

It is intriguing to me that violence and warfare require a suspension of belief in this basic doctrine. In order to harm or to kill a fellow human being, I must assume that he is basically foreign to me, an alien threat. Thus, for example, in wartime propaganda, there is an exaggerated emphasis on the racial and cultural difference of the enemy. During the Second World War, for example, British propagandists routinely referred to the Germans as the "Huns." This sort of rewiring of the mind is, in the deepest sense, a negation of the doctrine of creation. In our bones we feel our commonality with all things in the energy of God, and we know that this relationship is more basic and more enduring than any of the differences that separate us. It takes an enormous effort of the will and a tremendous amount of sinful cultural conditioning to knock this "creation consciousness" out of our hearts.

When Jesus speaks in the Sermon on the Mount of radical nonviolence, of turning the other cheek, of going the extra mile, he is not simply giving ethical suggestions. Rather, as we hinted above, he is trying to root his listeners in a creation spirituality. I ought to offer the other cheek to my persecutor because I realize, despite the violence, a far more enduring and powerful bond between us. The turning of the cheek expresses my celebration of this commonality, and one can hope that it will shame my persecutor into a similar recognition. The "ethics" of the Sermon on the Mount is a dramatic expression of the creation mentality in and through provocative action; it is a playing out of the mind and heart that have risen above the corrupting influence of sin and have seen the truth of things. It is a holding up of the icon of creation to a world in forgetfulness.

I would like to draw out another implication of this creation doctrine for the life of prayer. It was Thomas Merton who wrote that the heart of contemplative prayer is the discovery of that center where one is here and now being created by God.[16] By "center," Merton means not some aspect of one's person but that deepest place, that ground that underlies and encompasses all of one's being. It is that "dearest freshness deep down" where God is continually pouring forth the newness of being. To pray, in the deepest and fullest sense, is to live out of that place, to immerse oneself in it habitually, to become at home there. It is neither an activity of the mind, nor a movement of the will, nor a play of the imagination. Indeed, all of those functions take place at relatively superficial

---

15. Francis of Assisi, "The Canticle of Brother Sun," in *Francis and Clare: The Complete Works*, trans. Regis J. Armstrong and Ignatius C. Brady (Mahwah, NJ: Paulist, 1982), 37–39.

16. Thomas Merton, *Contemplative Prayer* (New York: Image Books, 1996), 5–6.

levels of the soul. To pray is to find that deep and serene pool that underlies and informs all that we are and do. It is to rest in it, to "sink into it," to affirm one's identity with it. What Merton is describing is, in Thomistic terms, a discovery, at the deepest possible level, of one's creatureliness.

Creation and Evil

Like all Christian theologians, like all celebrators of the encompassing power of the Creator God, Thomas Aquinas faces a grave problem: How does one explain the pervasive and devastating presence of evil in the world? If the gracious God is the one from whom being is continually flowing out into the universe, if the gentle God is the one found at the center of all things, why is there so much darkness, so much failure, so much tragedy? It is especially in our time, living in the aftermath of the bloodiest and most destructive of centuries, that this question takes on a particular pointedness. One can immediately see the spiritual danger that one faces even in posing this problem: the overwhelming force of evil can easily lead one to conclude that there are two basic principles at work in the world, a positive divine power and a malign demonic power. One's spiritual life can then become a dreadful combat, a battle whose outcome is never sure. One can feel torn between the equally powerful forces of dark and light. It is just this sort of destructive dualism that Thomas endeavors to avoid in his discussion of evil. He does so by showing in various ways that the goodness of God, which is indeed the ground of all there is, can sometimes present a dark face. Evil, he says again and again, is not a counter-principle to God but rather one of the subtle devices that God uses to work his purpose out, one of the somber colors that he uses in painting his variegated canvas.

In article 6 of question 3 of the *De potentia*, Aquinas tackles this problem directly.[17] In light of the fact of evil he wonders whether God can be seen as the sole principle of all that there is. The biblical icon of the *Sed contra*, which broods over the entire discussion, is one of the most deeply mysterious in all of Scripture. Thomas cites the prophet Isaiah: "I am the Lord and there is no other. I form light and create darkness, I make weal and create woe, it is I the Lord who do all this" (Isa. 45:5–7). Strangely, paradoxically, the all-good God is responsible for both weal and woe, for both triumph and calamity. What Isaiah implies, and what Thomas will make more conceptually precise, is that the goodness of

---

17. Thomas Aquinas, *The Power of God* 3.6.

God is far richer and much more complex than we customarily imagine. It is a fundamentally positive force that is great enough to encompass what appear to our limited vision as mutually exclusive principles.

Much misunderstanding comes, says Aquinas, from a failure to appreciate the nature of evil. Since evil weighs on us with such insistence and inspires such terror in us, it is easy to see it as a powerful force in its own right, as something that counterbalances the good. Without denying for a moment the *psychological* importance of evil, Thomas does deny emphatically that evil is *metaphysically* substantive:

> Now we have said above that good is everything appetible; and thus, since every nature desires its own being and its own perfection, it must be said also that the being and the perfection of any nature is good. Hence it cannot be that evil signifies being, or any form or nature. Therefore it must be that by the name of evil is signified the absence of good. And this is what is meant by saying that evil is *neither a being nor a good.*[18]

Evil is, in one sense, altogether "real" because it strikes us psychologically and spiritually; but, in the strict sense, it does not exist at all. What Thomas means is that evil is a privation or deprivation of the good, the absence of some good that ought to be present. Thus, we say it is evil if a human being is blind, since sight belongs to the nature of a human being, but we would never describe a sightless rock as evil. For Aquinas, evil is not a thing or a power that confronts the good; rather, it is a cavity, a vacuum, a lack, a corruption.

It would therefore be absurd to say that there is a purely evil principle or agent that actively confronts and challenges the creative power of God. Pure evil *cannot exist*, since evil can exist only as a sort of parasite on the good, only as a "wound" on something positive. The good is always more basic, more enduring, more powerful than evil. It is interesting that in traditional theology the devil is in no sense a counter-principle to God, a coequal power of sheer evil. On the contrary, the devil is metaphysically good, a being endowed with tremendous powers and virtues, who has tragically fallen into corruption. In no sense threatened by the devil or forced into a life-and-death struggle with him, God uses the devil when he wants for the working out of his good purposes.

All of this rather arcane discussion is, as we hinted above, of spiritual significance. One of the gravest dangers—and serious temptations—for the sinner is to find refuge from God through the identification with evil itself. In my pastoral practice, I have encountered this tendency frequently. A person finds

---

18. *Summa theologiae* 1.48.1.

himself caught in the web of some evil—be it an addiction, a self-destructive lifestyle, an obsessive pattern, a cycle of jealousy and violence—and, despite his best intentions and most concerted efforts, almost despite himself, he remains caught, fascinated by the chains that bind him. His soul-sickness is this: he is seeking escape from the press and demand of God precisely in what seems most opposed to God, precisely in evil itself. He is looking for a counter-principle, a dark god, in whose kingdom he can rest; he is looking for an oasis where he can find relief from the bright sun of God's presence.

Thomas' clarification of the nature of evil is a deft bit of spiritual direction. By affirming that evil does not exist, Thomas is not denying the spiritual power of evil, but he is telling the sinner that there is no place to run. Even in a full and radical embrace of evil, the sinner is still—stubbornly and, for him, frustratingly—in the greater context of the good. There is no finally evil place, since all places are, as such, good; and there is no finally evil attitude, since all attitudes, as such, are good. There is no totally evil kingdom, since any kingdom, even the worst, is fundamentally good.

This bit of metaphysical clarification is, of course, maddening to the sinner who wants desperately to find a route of escape from God. It is also, at the same time, an invitation to salvation, since it convinces the sinner that in standing on evil he stands on shadows and mists. In hurling himself into the darkness of sin and corruption, he discovers not some great counter-principle to God but only a vacuum, from which God will ultimately summon him. Thomas' doctrine of evil as nonbeing is a call to surrender to the good that cannot, in any final sense, be avoided.

Here I am reminded of Hans Urs von Balthasar's discussion of the overwhelming salvific power of God. God's outreach of love is so intense, his compassion so tireless and efficacious, says Balthasar, that he will eventually wear down even the most stubborn of sinners. Eventually, we can hope, God's wily and indefatigable love will trick even the cleverest sinner out of his self-imposed prison of illusion.[19] To be sure, we must believe that, given the fact of freedom, a human being could in a final sense say no to God, but we must at the same time reasonably hope that all people will eventually be outwitted by the benign trickery of divine love.

---

19. See Hans Urs von Balthasar, *Dare We Hope "That All Men Be Saved"?* 2nd ed., trans. David Kipp and Lothar Krauth (San Francisco: Ignatius Press, 2014), 163–168.

In sum, a healthy creation spirituality knows that good is the substance and evil the shadow or, in G.K. Chesterton's words, "that this is a white world with black spots, not a black world with white spots."[20]

If, therefore, evil is not a substance—not a thing but only a lack—it follows that neither God nor any other principle *creates* evil. It is more accurate to say, according to Thomas, that God *permits* this darkness in creation. But this leads him, and us, inevitably to the question "Why?" Granted that God does not directly produce evil, why does he nevertheless allow it to have such free rein, such destructive power in the world? Can we finally reconcile the fact of devastating evil with a God who is filled with wisdom and benevolence? Does not the very presence of suffering and evil prove, as David Hume argued, that God cannot be all-knowing, all-loving, and all-powerful?[21] For indeed, it seems that if God knew about evil (in his omniscience), if he wanted to rid the world of it (in his omnibenevolence), and if he could do something about it (in his omnipotence), there would be no evil. Does the existence of evil not demonstrate, in Woody Allen's phrase, that God is, at best, an underachiever?[22]

As Thomas Aquinas works through his subtle response to this vexing question, we find a way to enter into the experience of evil as part of the drama of redemption. We discover how to accept suffering and negativity themselves, not as signs of God's absence or weakness, but rather as indications of his ever-greater and ever-more-mysterious love.

It is in responding to the fourth objection to article 6 of question 3 of the *De potentia* that Thomas answers the kind of argument that Hume and others have formulated over the centuries. It is worth quoting Aquinas here at some length:

> It is due to neither impotence nor ignorance on God's part that evils occur in the world, but it is owing to the order of his wisdom and to the greatness of his goodness, whence come the many and diverse grades of goodness in things, many of which would be lacking were he to allow no evil to exist. Thus, there would be no good of patience without the evil of persecution, nor the good of the preservation of its life in a lion, without the evil of the destruction of the animals on which it lives.[23]

---

20. G.K. Chesterton, "Tolerating Other Religions," in *Collected Works*, vol. 29, *The Illustrated London News: 1911–1913*, ed. Lawrence J. Clipper (San Francisco: Ignatius Press, 1990), 500–503.

21. David Hume, *Dialogues Concerning Natural Religion*, ed. Dorothy Coleman (Cambridge: Cambridge University Press, 2007), 74.

22. *Love and Death*, directed by Woody Allen (Beverly Hills, CA: United Artists, 1975).

23. Thomas Aquinas, *The Power of God* 3.6 ad. 4.

In the *Summa*, Thomas makes this same point more directly by saying that God "allows evils to happen in order to bring a greater good therefrom."[24]

Admittedly, in light of the truly monstrous evils experienced in our time, this argument can seem on the face of it rather facile, even a little callous. Indeed, it seems hard to find the "greater good" that flowed from the Holocaust or that might come about as a result of the stockpiling of nuclear weapons, but let us attend carefully to Thomas' examples, especially the last. The good of preserving life in the lion could not possibly exist were it not for the evil of destroying the lives of the hundreds of animals on which the lion lives. Given the limitations of its own biological structure and environment, the predator could not realize the good of its continuing existence without entering into conflict with, and finally devouring, other creatures, without causing enormous suffering and loss. What Thomas signals here is the *essentially conflictual nature of finitude itself*. A world of finite things is, necessarily, a world in tension. Thus, for example, to achieve the perfection of knowledge, I must choose not to pursue an infinity of other possible goods; to have the pleasure of being in a given place, I must choose not to be in a thousand other places; my having a particular job implies that dozens of others, who wanted the same job, are disappointed; in order that I might live, plants and animals must die; etc. The point is that evil seems to be a regrettable, but necessary, product of finitude, an unavoidable element of creatureliness. In the light of this clarification, we can better understand God's "permission" of evil to bring about a greater good. It is not as though God arbitrarily decides to "allow" suffering and darkness (as if he could have avoided it); rather, in *deciding* to *create*, in deciding to make a finite world at all, God accepted the inevitability of conflict and evil. Thus, even with regard to the unspeakable horror of the Holocaust, one is obliged to say, however painfully, that God permits this monstrous abuse of free will in order to allow free will itself to exist.

An image that has helped me understand this great mystery—and one that is reverenced by our tradition—is that of the parent. When a mother decides to bring a child into the world, she must, if she is at all reflective, feel in advance the myriad pains that her son or daughter will inevitably suffer. She knows that her child will be frequently disappointed, will endure insults and barbed remarks, will become at various times terribly sick, will perhaps lose a beloved wife or friend, will, in short, face all of the enormities and calamities of a normal human life. Yet she decides to give birth. Why? Because she is convinced that the beauty and ecstasy of human life is *worth all of this unavoidable suffering*. She permits this evil in order that the greater good of life itself might be realized. The creator

---

24. *Summa theologiae* 3.1.3 ad. 3.

God is father and mother, author of life and being. Does God weep in the face of the pain of his creation? Undoubtedly yes. But like the good parent, God permits this negativity that the beauty of creation itself might emerge. With resignation and, we can imagine, a certain anguish, God accepts the evil that will inevitably follow from the decision to create.

Thomas' example of the lion devouring its prey illustrates not only the conflictual nature of finitude but also the relativity of evil. The blessing for the lion—finding and consuming food to preserve its life—is an unspeakable curse for the poor antelope or wildebeest that it eats. It is easy to forget this principle, especially when it comes to evils that we human beings suffer. Thus, we speak, legitimately, of the terrible negativity that is cancer, but we overlook the fact that this evil appears so only *for us and from our perspective*. Though it sounds ludicrous, it is correct to say that, while the cancer cells are destroying a healthy human body, they are, from their point of view, flourishing. And the great goods (from our perspective) of cancer surgery or chemotherapy are (from the perspective of the tumor) unmitigated evils. Similarly, the earthquake, which levels a city and takes thousands of lives, is from the geological standpoint simply a release of pressure, an inevitable and in itself harmless process of nature.

Now, these observations are not meant to deny the power and horror of the evils we suffer, but they are intended to place evil itself in a broader, indeed cosmic, perspective. Thomas seems to be urging us to see good and evil not simply from our narrow human angle but, as far as we can, from God's all-embracing perspective:

> To those . . . who estimate things, not by the nature thereof, but by the good they themselves can derive therefrom, everything that is harmful to themselves seems simply evil. For they do not reflect [on the fact] that what is in some way injurious to one person, to another is beneficial, and that even to themselves the same thing may be evil in some respects but good in others.[25]

Interestingly, the spiritual strategy here is very similar to that employed by Yahweh in the book of Job. Overwhelmed, understandably, by his terrible personal sufferings, Job cries out to God to justify himself, to make sense of what appears to Job as meaningless and undeserved pain. Speaking out of the desert whirlwind, God does not address himself directly to Job's suffering or his moral dilemma. Rather, he presents a magnificent catalogue of his strangest and most impressive natural creations, drawing special attention to the Leviathan, the monster that patrols the depths. In a word, Yahweh *expands the consciousness* of

---

25. *Summa theologiae* 1.65.1 ad. 2.

Job, forcing him out of his constrained and anthropocentric take on his suffering. He compels his servant to understand what is happening to him against the backdrop of the infinite and mysterious cosmos that is, as much as Job himself, part of God's concern. To be sure, neither the author of the book of Job nor Thomas Aquinas is denying the intensity of personal suffering, but both, it seems to me, are inviting the sufferer to a more Godlike vision of suffering itself.

Creation and Beauty

Toward the end of his early novel *A Portrait of the Artist as a Young Man*, James Joyce presents a lively conversation between the protagonist, Stephen Dedalus, and his friend Lynch. What the two brilliant Irish students discuss is something we might not expect. They are engaged in a detailed analysis of Thomas Aquinas' doctrine of beauty.[26] This scholastic understanding of the beautiful was to have a lifelong influence on Joyce, expressing for him his deepest sense of vocation and purpose. The medieval theologian articulated for the twentieth-century novelist the ideal that would preoccupy and fascinate him for the whole of his life: noticing and describing epiphanies, moments when the beautiful shines forth in its peculiar clarity and power.

More often than not, Aquinas discusses the beautiful in the context of creation and God's purpose in creating. One of his favorite descriptions of the Creator God—one that appears throughout his writings—is that of God as artist or craftsman, and one of his most consistent images for the created realm is that of artifact or beautiful object. As we saw above, Thomas is well aware of the corruption and ugliness that can invade God's creation, but he was fully convinced that not even the greatest darkness could mar the underlying beauty, order, and harmony that he perceived and celebrated everywhere in the universe. I would like, then, to complete this study of Thomas' creation doctrine by looking closely at the topic of beauty, a subject too often overlooked in more rationalist considerations of the Angelic Doctor.

What is it that compels us to call something "beautiful"? For Thomas, it is not simply a question of subjective impression or private opinion. There is, he thinks, an objectivity to beauty; there is something in an object or person that calls out to us and captivates us. He describes the nature of the beautiful in

---

26. James Joyce, *A Portrait of the Artist as a Young Man* (Mineola, NY: Dover, 1994), 134–163.

various ways in his writings, but the qualities that he most commonly specifies as essential to beauty are *consonantia* (harmony) and *claritas* (luminosity).

> He shows in what the *ratio* of beauty consists, adding that God so hands on beauty, inasmuch as he is *the cause of the consonance and clarity* in all things: for thus we call a man beautiful, on account of seemly proportion in quantity and position and on account of the fact that he has a clear and shining color. Whence it must be received proportionally in the rest of things, that each is called beautiful according as it has clarity of its kind, whether spiritual or bodily, and according as it is constituted in due proportion.[27]

When the harmony of a thing becomes luminous, when its inner coherence and organization shine forth, the beautiful emerges. Thus, a natural scene—say a mountain view—is particularly beautiful when the arrangement of shapes and textures and the play of colors is strikingly harmonious and pleasant to contemplate. Some months ago, I was watching a football game on television, and the camera caught a burly lineman standing along the sidelines, having just come out of action. His jersey was ripped, there was mud and blood on his face, his hair was wildly unkempt, and his battered helmet was held jauntily under his arm. As he contemplated this figure, one of the announcers said, "Now, there's a beauty!" At first, I was taken aback at this rather surprising comment, but then I realized that his reaction was perfectly understandable in light of Aquinas' principles. For what he saw in that disheveled lineman was a luminous coming together of those qualities of courage, physical strength, and reckless abandon that for him define a football player. That announcer was held in what James Joyce, following Thomas Aquinas, called aesthetic "arrest," a state of enraptured wonder.[28] It is this condition of the soul that is produced by the light and harmony of the beautiful.

Thomas' basic attitude in the presence of God's creation is one of aesthetic arrest. He seems perpetually overwhelmed, entranced by the order and harmony, by the brilliant organization that surrounds him. Indeed, one of the surest signs of the divine presence is just this stunning beauty:

> Suppose a person entering a house were to feel heat on the porch, and going further, were to feel the heat increasing, the more he penetrated within. Doubtless, he would believe there was a fire in the house, even though he did not see the fire that must be causing all this heat. A similar thing will happen to anyone who considers this world in detail: he will observe that all things

---

27. Thomas Aquinas, *Commentary on Dionysius' On the Divine Names* 4.5.339.
28. James Joyce, *A Portrait of the Artist as a Young Man*, 148–149.

are arranged according to their degrees of beauty and excellence, and that the nearer they are to God, the more beautiful and the better they are.[29]

What this charming quotation shows is Thomas' appreciation of the dizzying display of beauty and light (as well as heat!) that appears when one simply opens one's eyes and looks. The universe is, as John Calvin put it some centuries later, a theater for the glory of God.[30] Though the full beauty of the producer is unavailable to us, increasingly intense signs of his artistic touch are visible everywhere on the stage and in the action of the play.

Though I will speak of it more thoroughly in the last chapter, it might be appropriate to say just a word at this point about contemplation. For Thomas Aquinas, the highest expression of the human soul, the greatest accomplishment of the human person, is *contemplatio*, a wonder-filled, ecstatic absorption in the beauty of God.[31] It should be obvious that Aquinas' attitude toward the created universe is contemplative. Unlike his modern successors, who will be concerned above all with the mastery of nature through knowledge, Thomas is a mystic, someone who gazes at the loveliness of the world in an attitude of prayer. For Thomas, the world in its totality is a sort of icon of the divine beauty, a mirror in which we see reflected some of the unbearable perfection of the divine being. Thus, the contemplation of the world constitutes a foretaste of the beatific vision, the blissful and unobstructed seeing of God, which is our fulfillment in heaven.

It is also through an appeal to beauty that Thomas endeavors to solve a problem that has vexed philosophers and theologians down through the ages— namely, why and how would the supremely one and simple God have given rise to a universe that is so wildly and richly pluralistic, so characterized by diversity and variety? Indeed, the ancient philosopher Plotinus maintains that the supremely unique God does not directly create the fantastically diverse world that we know. On the contrary, he does so through a hierarchy of intermediaries, which acts as a sort of buffer assuring that the splendid unity of the divine is not contaminated by contact with the grossly plural physical world.

Thomas Aquinas could not be in stronger disagreement with Plotinus on this score. As we have seen, the Creator God is intimately connected to each thing in the universe: he is the intimate source of the being of rocks as well as angels.

---

29. Thomas Aquinas, *The Apostles' Creed*, in *The Three Greatest Prayers: Commentaries on the Lord's Prayer, the Hail Mary, and the Apostles' Creed*, trans. Laurence Shapcote (Manchester, NH: Sophia Institute, 1990), 13–14.

30. John Calvin, *A Commentary on the Psalms of David* 135:13–14, (Oxford: D.A. Talboys, 1840), 3:396.

31. See *Summa theologiae* 1-2.3.7 ad. 3, 1-2.3.5, and 2-2.180.4: "contemplation is the end of the whole human life."

God is not closer to any one creature than to another; rather, he is infinitely and equally close to them all. Thomas sees the plural universe not as something unworthy of God but rather as the explosive and creative expression of the wild fullness of the divine beauty:

> Because his goodness could not be adequately represented by one creature alone, [God] produced many and diverse creatures, that what was wanting in one in the representation of the divine goodness might be supplied by another. For goodness, which in God is simple and uniform, in creatures is manifold and divided, and hence the whole universe together participates in the divine goodness more perfectly and represents it better than any single creature whatever.[32]

Why does God continually create the billions of stars, the eerie vastness of interstellar space, the myriad cratered moons, the thousands of species of fish, the infinitely varying winds, the stunning range of colors in the wings of birds, the countless single-celled organisms, the almost frightening complexity of a single human brain? And why did God once give rise to civilizations come and gone, to the ferocious and magnificent Tyrannosaurus Rex, to the beautiful plants now remembered only through fossils? Why does God make the sun to rise again and again? Because he is an extravagant child who never tires of play. Or to use Andrew Greeley's even more apt metaphor, because he is a teenager caught up in the sheer exuberance of his creativity and sense of the possible.[33] Why does a teenager dye her hair in outlandish colors and wear clothes that shock the members of polite society? For much the same reason, I imagine, as God creates toucans and giraffes: for the fun of it—and perhaps even for its shock value.

In more Thomistic language, God engages in this explosive and irrepressible creativity because he is determined to show, as fully as possible, some of the intensity of his own beauty. No one creature could ever demonstrate the splendor of God; indeed, no million or trillion creatures could do so. But God never tires of trying. God is like a concentration of pure light that—in creation—passes through a prism and is then reflected and refracted in a fantastic array of hues. Each creature is a piece of a mosaic designed to depict the fullness of the divine glory, a thread woven into a tapestry reflective of God's beauty.

---

32. *Summa theologiae* 1.47.1.

33. See, for instance, Andrew M. Greeley, *Sacraments of Love: A Prayer Journal* (New York: Crossroad, 1994), 68.

Conclusion

It is my conviction that Thomas Aquinas' teaching on creation is, at the same time, the most powerful and most overlooked dimension of his doctrine. When we attend to him carefully on this score, we discover something marvelous and wholly unexpected: the basic energy of the created realm is a relationship of love. God continually pours out the gift of being, and the world is at every moment a sheer receptivity, an openness toward that gift. Human beings are in a privileged position because they are able to perceive and to celebrate this relationship that they are. Indeed, at the heart of the spiritual life, for Aquinas, is this struggle to *see authentically who we are* in relation to the God who perpetually offers us "newness of being." When we realize, in imitation of Christ, that we are "nothing" in the presence of the creating God, we become "everything," a full reflection of the divine glory. Sin is thus a sort of illusion, a stubborn clinging to falsehood, an insistence that we stand over and against God, the supreme being. Let go of yourself, implies Thomas, in an ecstatic acceptance of creatureliness, and you will find the security that you so long for. In the face of your greatest fears, give yourself away.

When we grasp the reality of creation, we see that the divisions between the "sacred" and the "profane," between the holy and the secular are, for the most part, arbitrary and misleading. All reality is sacred, from the angels to subatomic particles, because all things are equally close to the creator God who dwells in every aspect of being. The sacramental imagination, which sees the divine lurking in every corner of the real, is fed and strengthened by the Thomistic doctrine of creation.

As we saw, even the profoundest expressions of evil cannot shake our confidence in this intoxicating vision. Though psychologically overwhelming, evil should never be spiritually debilitating, since we appreciate it against the ever-greater background of God's gift of being. With eyes cleansed and purified by the revelation contained in Christ Jesus, we can see the divine beauty everywhere in creation; we can appreciate the light and harmony that are sacraments of the perfect luminosity and orderliness of the Creator God.

Chapter Four

THE HUMAN BEING:
MADE FOR ECSTASY

I t is often remarked that the Renaissance represented a rebirth of humanism after the long medieval emphasis on asceticism and other-worldliness. With the great sculptors, painters, and scholars of the sixteenth century, the argument goes, the human being, in all of his Godlike splendor, moves center stage. Just think for a moment of the beautiful and adept figures that populate Michelangelo's Sistine Chapel ceiling, or of the magnificent humanity that is celebrated in Leonardo's *Last Supper*. These classic works signify, it is said, a clear departure from the pessimism, dualism, and spiritualism of the Middle Ages and express a renewed appreciation for the integral human being—body and soul, flesh and spirit.

I have always found this point of view puzzling. The strongest and most influential philosophical voice of the Renaissance was undoubtedly that of Plato. Young Michelangelo, for instance, picked up his Platonism at the court of his patron, Lorenzo de Medici, and his mature work, including the Sistine ceiling, is redolent of the Platonic spirit. But Plato was, of course, the greatest dualist of the tradition, the philosopher who put perhaps strongest emphasis on the struggle against the flesh and who most dramatically stated that the human being is essentially spirit trapped in matter.[1] This philosophical principle can be seen, in strikingly beautiful form, in the so-called Captives that Michelangelo sculpted for the tomb of Pope Julius II. These figures twist and writhe in their battle to be free of the encumbrance of the flesh; they represent the drive of the spirit away from matter toward union with God.

---

1. See Plato, *Cratylus* 400c, *Phaedo* 51e–62c, *Gorgias* 493a, *Republic* 586a, and *Phaedrus* 520c: "That was the ultimate vision, and we saw it in pure light because we were pure ourselves, not buried in this thing we are carrying around now, which we call a body, locked in it like an oyster in its shell" (trans. Alexander Nehamas and Paul Woodruff, in *Plato: Complete Works*, ed. John M. Cooper and D.S. Hutchinson [Indianapolis, IN: Hackett, 1997], 528).

But the most influential philosopher of the supposedly anti-humanist Middle Ages—and the one who was of decisive importance for Thomas Aquinas—was Aristotle. And it was Aristotle who pointedly disagreed with the dualism of Plato, affirming again and again the fundamental unity of the human being, the coming together of body and soul in an inseparable harmony. In fact, when this radical doctrine made its way into the Christian world in the thirteenth century, it was immediately condemned as irreconcilable with belief in the immortality of the soul. But it was this pro-body, this-worldly doctrine of Aristotle that young Thomas embraced with enthusiasm and never stopped defending even in the face of violent opposition. Thomas will say throughout his writings that the human being—precisely as a unity of spirit and matter—is a beautiful reflection of the divine and a creature destined for deification. So close is the rapport between flesh and spirit that even in the rapture of the beatific vision the human soul will be unsatisfied until it is reunited with the body.

There were undoubtedly dualist and anti-humanist doctrines in the Middle Ages—witness for example some of the works of St. Bernard of Clairvaux—but the teachings of the greatest medieval doctor, who is the subject of this book, are anything but dualist. In fact—and this is the great irony—they are far more humanist than much of the art of the Renaissance. Thomas' thought is a celebration of the human, a consistent and thorough reiteration of St. Irenaeus' adage that "the glory of God is a human being fully alive."[2]

In this chapter, we shall consider Thomas' view of the human person. A union of spirit and matter, the human being is made in the image of God and destined for the glorious transforming vision of the divine power. From the beginning of his life and to the roots of his being the human is touched by a divine energy that lures him to self-transcendence. Thomas' anthropology is anything but static; on the contrary, it is centered upon the assumption that we are dynamically constituted, that we are, if you will, built for ecstasy, for the movement outward toward God. The human spirit, for Thomas, is "wired" for a spiritual journey upward toward the divine source. We are hunger and thirst for God; we are a longing, a striving for completeness; we are a passion for vision. As we have seen throughout this book, human beings are designed for union with the creative source of all that is. We are made for bliss and for light and for the ecstatic realization of our nothingness before God.

And of course in all of this we can see the centrality of the icon of Jesus Christ. Thomas understands God, the world, creation, nature, *and the human being* in light of that overwhelming experience we have spoken of so often in

---

2. Irenaeus, *Against Heresies* 4.20.7, in *Catechism of the Catholic Church* 294.

this book: the shock of the Incarnation. Aquinas reads the human off of the paradigmatic humanity of Jesus himself. And Jesus in his concrete humanity is, as we have seen, nothing but a sheer openness to transcendence.

Oneness of the Human Being

It is extremely difficult for us to appreciate the importance and novelty of Thomas Aquinas' understanding of the unity of the human. The biblical notion of the intimate connection between body and spirit had largely been forgotten as Christianity moved into the world of Hellenistic philosophy. In the thought of Origen, Gregory of Nyssa, Augustine, Anselm, and so many other of the most influential Christian theologians, the dominant philosophical pattern was that of Plato and his followers. In Christianized form, this Platonism appeared in an emphasis upon the sharp distinction between soul and body.

For many of the great Christian spiritual masters prior to Aquinas, there is, to some degree, a suspicion of the body, a tendency to view the flesh as an obstacle to the ascent of the spirit. In his wonderful book *Civilisation*, Lord Kenneth Clark shows us an illuminated manuscript from the tenth century that includes a portrait of a man. So little stress was placed on the accurate depiction of the body of this figure that the illuminator felt obliged to write over it *imago hominis*, an image of a man.[3] This sort of "bracketing" of the body as spiritually irrelevant was typical of a hyper-Platonized Christianity. A belief in the immortality of the soul seemed to many of these thinkers to require a clear demarcation between the purely immaterial mind and the body destined for death and dissolution. It was one of the principle innovations of Aquinas to show that this dualism is itself a major source of mischief and a block to authentic spiritual development. It is only when we human beings fully acknowledge that we are good precisely as God made us that we can relate properly to the Creator.

In many of his writings, Thomas insists that the soul is not a thing separate from the body but is rather the "form" of the body. It is most important to understand what he means by this. In saying that the soul informs the body, Aquinas implies that the spirit is the unifying and organizing energy by which a particular conglomeration of bone, flesh, and nerve becomes properly human. As such, the spirit is not a self-contained and self-sufficient ghostly substance

---

3. Kenneth Clark, *Civilisation: A Personal View* (New York: Harper & Row, 1969), 11.

that mysteriously and temporarily unites itself to a body. On the contrary, it is intimately tied to and oriented toward the body that it contains and animates.

> As it belongs to the notion of this particular man to be composed of this soul, of this flesh, and of these bones; so it belongs to the notion of man to be composed of soul, flesh and bones.[4]

So tight is the interrelationship between spirit and flesh that, when we define the human being, the two cannot be separated out. It is decidedly not the case that the human being is essentially or basically a soul that has an incidental relation to a body or that, in Plato's language, merely "uses" a body. For Thomas, "the whole human soul is in the whole body, and again, in every part, as God is in regard to the whole world."[5]

This is a wonderful comparison. Just as God is no closer to the angel than to the rock, just as God immediately and creatively fills every corner of the universe, so the soul is intimately and fully present to all expressions of bodiliness, to all sensation, to all feeling. There is nothing in the body that is unworthy of the soul or beneath its dignity; rather, the soul enters into all bodily functions and expressions, energizing and enlivening them.

Accordingly, we ought not to consider the body as an obstacle to the soul, a weight holding it down, preventing it from making its spiritual ascent to God:

> Now the nature of our body was created, not by an evil principle, as the Manicheans pretend, but by God. . . . Consequently, out of the love of charity with which we love God, we ought to love our bodies also.[6]

Several times in his writings Thomas shows his impatience with Origen's view that the soul was united to a body as a sort of punishment for sin.[7] This theory, he thinks, flies in the face not only of the biblical witness that God made all things good but also of the philosophical intuition, so deeply felt by Aquinas, that soul and body belong together. Were bodiliness a penalty for sin, the soul would continually chafe against the flesh (as in Michelangelo's sculptures), longing to be rid of it. But for Aquinas just the opposite is the case: the soul is most itself and most at home in a body, or better, "with" a body. Against Origen, Thomas Aquinas says that we ought to celebrate the wonderful communion of body and soul.

The implications of this radical view for the spiritual life are profound. First, we must make peace with our bodies. The theoretical dualism of our tradition

---

4. Thomas Aquinas, *Summa theologiae* 1.75.4.
5. *Summa theologiae* 1.93.3.
6. *Summa theologiae* 2-2.25.5.
7. See, for instance, Thomas Aquinas, *Disputed Questions on the Soul* 2 ad. 14.

has had some devastating practical consequences, forcing people to be suspicious of pleasure, of the instinctual life, of the sensations associated with sexuality. Especially in those cultures marked by puritanical forms of Protestantism or Jansenist Catholicism, there is a tendency to demonize the body and its passions as necessarily "fallen," as inimical to the purposes of God. That the body and its pleasures might be intertwined with the "things of the spirit" is unthinkable to the dualist.

But to Thomas Aquinas, such intermingling is undeniable and, in fact, worthy of celebration. Let us listen to the Dominican master as he speaks, in a decidedly nondualist way, of the sexual impulse:

> Natural inclinations are implanted in things by God, who moves all things. Therefore, the natural inclination of a species cannot be to that which is evil in itself. Now, in all perfect animals there is a natural inclination toward carnal intercourse. Therefore, carnal intercourse cannot possibly be evil in itself.[8]

He even states that the sensible delight that comes from sexual intercourse was greater in paradise than it is now.[9] Fresh from the hand of God, the human being was, if anything, sexier than she is at present, sin having diminished some of the "sensibility of the body." It is absolutely not the case for Thomas Aquinas that pleasure and carnality in themselves are signs of, or inducements toward, sin—quite the contrary. Sin has only rendered the bodily passions disordered and hence less intense, less deeply satisfying. The human ideal is hardly a disembodied spirituality, but rather an enspirited bodiliness, a sensuality in union with the proper impulse toward love and nurturance.

The inseparable unity of body and soul also has implications for how we know and relate to God. In so many philosophies and spiritualities, the intensity of one's knowledge of God depends upon the completeness of one's separation from the flesh. One of the greatest pagan influences on Christian spirituality was the Platonic philosopher Plotinus, who was described by his biographer as someone who "seemed ashamed of being in the body."[10]

For Plotinus, the heart of the spiritual life is an ascent away from this world, away from particularity and multiplicity, away, above all, from the encumbrance of matter toward a union with the One who is the source of all existence. "A flight of the alone to the Alone" in a purely intellectual rapture is for this Platonist

---

8. Thomas Aquinas, *Summa contra Gentiles* 3.126.3.

9. *Summa theologiae* 1.98.2 ad. 3.

10. *Porphyry: On the Life of Plotinus and the Arrangement of His Work*, in *Plotinus: The Enneads*, trans. Stephen MacKenna, rev. B.S. Page (London: Faber, 1956), 1.

the summit of human experience.[11] Once again, Thomas could not be in more dramatic disagreement with this sort of spiritualism.

First, for Aquinas, the knowledge of God comes through the senses, through the mediation of the body. As we saw in chapter 1, the great and unsurpassable disclosure of God's love takes place in the Incarnation, in the enfleshment of the Son of God. Thomas would make his own the words of the first letter of John: "We declare to you what was from the beginning, what we have heard, what we have seen with our eyes, what we have looked at and touched with our hands, concerning the word of life" (1 John 1:1). God's being and intention are revealed in the bodily event of the Incarnation and are literally *seen* and *heard* with the lowly senses. For Aquinas, one does not flee from matter to arrive at God; rather, one immerses oneself in the matter that God has sanctified and through which God deigns to disclose himself. Furthermore, our indirect philosophical knowledge of God comes, similarly, through bodily contact with the world. As we saw, it is through reflection on motion, causality, order, and beauty that we arrive at a vague understanding of God as the ground and Creator of all. For Thomas, the divine is appreciated *precisely in and through the world* that has been made by the divine power. In some of his least known but most provocative writings, Thomas reminds us in no uncertain terms that the highest activities of the human mind, its most soaring abstractions, even its rising to the height of contemplating God, are rooted in, and conditioned by, the body, the senses, and the imagination. The spirit does not leave matter behind in its "ascent" to the One; rather, it carries matter with it even to the throne of God.

This consistently incarnational spirituality is, to be sure, deeply Catholic. For Aquinas, we "know" the divine not through mystical elevation, not through infused wisdom, but through pictures, stories, colors, shapes, events, persons, and natural phenomena. There is, throughout his writings, what I would call a sacramental sensibility, a keen awareness of the embodiment of God in the world. There is in Thomas an interesting mix of what C.G. Jung would call the intuitional and the sensate.[12] On the one hand, Aquinas' writings are desperately abstract, soaringly philosophical in their attempt to see the whole, but this intuitive style is always balanced by and grounded in an appeal to direct and ordinary experience. There is something stubbornly earthy and commonsensical in Thomas' work, despite his flights of academic rhetoric. Josef Pieper, one of the

---

11. Plotinus, *The Enneads* 6.9.11, trans. Andrew Louth, in *The Origins of the Christian Mystical Tradition from Plato to Denys* (Oxford: Clarendon, 1983), 51.

12. Carl G. Jung, *Psychological Types*, trans. H.G. Baynes, rev. R.F.C. Hull, in *The Collected Works of C.G. Jung*, ed. Herbert Read et al., vol. 6 (Princeton, NJ: Princeton University Press, 1976), esp. chap. 11.

great Thomists of our century, recalls a conversation he had as a student with one of his philosophy professors. Young Pieper was filled with enthusiasm for the writings of Schelling and Hegel, the nineteenth-century German romantic idealists. The teacher smiled and said, "Well, that's fine confectionary sugar and cake frosting; it's tasty and beautiful, but not very good for you. Open the books of Thomas Aquinas and you will find some good brown bread, solid and nutritious." We see this brown-bread quality particularly in Aquinas' insistence upon the body and the senses in our knowledge of God.

The Thomistic emphasis upon the unity of body and soul is perhaps no more clearly and dramatically expressed than in Aquinas' treatment of the state of the blessed in heaven. In a later section of this chapter, I shall describe in greater detail Thomas' view of the experience of heaven, but for now I want simply to show that it is the whole human person, body and spirit, who enjoys the fullness of the vision of God. For Aquinas, paradise is no disembodied, purely intellectual state of affairs; on the contrary, it is richly imagined as the blissful fulfillment of the totality of human being:

> At the resurrection the soul will not resume a celestial or ethereal body, or the body of some animal. . . . No, it will resume a human body made up of flesh and bones, and equipped with the same organs it now possesses.[13]

In a word, it is I who am saved and not some aspect, some dimension of myself. It is I in my concrete humanity who aspire to God to achieve my hoped-for fulfillment. To be sure, Thomas Aquinas holds that the soul is, in itself, immaterial and hence immortal, but the soul is built for a body and remains, as it were, deeply unsatisfied without a body.

> Since, therefore, the natural human soul is naturally united to the body, . . . it has a natural desire for union with the body. Hence the will cannot be perfectly at rest until the soul is again joined to the body. . . . Therefore man's final happiness requires the soul to be again united to the body.[14]

The intense experience of God enjoyed by a disembodied soul is real but radically incomplete, since it lacks the corporeal "feel" that makes it distinctively human. In this life, a stunning vision or a beautiful thought produces a satisfying bodily reaction, an "e-motion," literally, a movement in the flesh. So the vision of God—if it is to be humanly complete—must involve the body to which the soul is so intimately connected.

---

13. Thomas Aquinas, *Compendium of Theology* 1.153.
14. *Compendium of Theology* 1.151.

Of course the heavenly body, though in continuity with the earthly flesh, is different precisely because it is in such close harmony with the soul. It is as though the clarity and simplicity of the soul "shines through" the resurrected body, giving it a new spiritualized quality:

> Holding the body completely under its sway, the soul will render the body subtle and spiritual. The soul will also bestow on the body a most noble quality, namely, the radiant beauty of clarity. . . . As a tool is to him who plies it, [the body] will be endowed with agility.[15]

That last image is powerful. Many musicians comment that when they are deeply involved in the music, there is a sort of symbiosis between them and their instruments. So great is this feeling of unity, they say, that the instrument "plays them." One of the characteristics of our sinful existence is a disharmony between body and soul, a loss of attunement between flesh and spirit. Indeed, one could argue that so much of the dualism that has plagued our tradition has its roots precisely in this *sinful* state of affairs, this regrettable but undeniable tension between body and soul. In our egotism and fear, the body does in fact often seem an encumbrance to the soul, an instrument that remains stubbornly out of tune or unresponsive to the player. Heaven, for Thomas Aquinas, is that state of being in which the divinely sanctioned union of body and soul is fully realized, finally attained, a place where the beauty of one enhances and calls out to the beauty of the other.

Thomas expands upon this vision in the *Summa contra Gentiles,* where he argues that the resurrected flesh is free of all "corruption, deformity, and defect."[16] Also, the risen body, he thinks, will continue to take pleasure in the exercise of its senses, exulting in physical beauty. We notice once more that the physical is not left behind or bracketed in Thomas' understanding of heaven; rather, paradise, though it is beyond all particular places, must include somehow the characteristics of space and color and sound; it must be a condition in which human beings feel at home.

Now, I realize that some of this can strike us as rather naïve. Indeed, if we follow Thomas' discussion of heaven through to the end, we find some fanciful observations concerning the age and behavior of the blessed. But there is in Thomas' vision a healthy instinct that must be continually emphasized in the face of dualisms of all sorts. Thomas is convinced that the creation of the integral human being was not a mistake, but was rather an expression of God's

---

15. *Compendium of Theology* 1.168.
16. *Summa contra Gentiles* 4.86.4.

artistic creativity and ingenuity. God made us good—body and soul—and God thus intends that we live our lives and reach our final consummation precisely as embodied souls, or better, as ensouled bodies. From our more enlightened scientific perspective, it probably seems that Thomas is overstating the continuity between the earthly and the risen body, but we can, and must, it seems to me, respect his fundamental intuition that it is the whole person who, under the influence of God, moves to salvation.

The Human Being: *Imago Dei*

In speaking of the human person as the image of God, Thomas Aquinas joins a long and venerable theological tradition whose roots are ultimately biblical. The book of Genesis tells us that God created Adam in his own image and according to his likeness, thus establishing the special dignity of the human in distinction to the other creatures. In the patristic period, particularly in the writings of Gregory of Nyssa, Origen, and Augustine, this similarity between the divine and the human was greatly emphasized, the *imago Dei* emerging as the "spark" of God's life in each person, the orientation of the human being toward union with God. The *imago* is the central organizing principle in Bernard of Clairvaux's series of sermons on the Song of Songs, writings that were to have an incalculable influence on the development of the spiritual tradition through John of the Cross and beyond. The *imago Dei* is so important to theological and spiritual writers because it gives a sense of the possibility of union with the divine, which is the goal of all spiritual striving. If we are, to some degree, *like* God, we can aspire to taste and see the divine; if we have within us something like a spark of God's life, then we are not hopelessly exiled from the sacred presence, and our deepest hopes are then not in vain.

Like so many of his predecessors, Thomas sees the divine spark precisely in the dynamism of the human spirit. Following Aristotle, he says that the mind is "in a certain sense, all things," meaning thereby that the human spirit is capable of knowing and reaching out to all expressions of being.[17] There is a tremendous range to the mind, a limitless and restless curiosity. It is never satisfied simply knowing material things, but rather it pushes ever outward and upward, seeking to know the formal, the universal, the abstract, and the spiritual.

---

17. *Summa theologiae* 1.14.1.

The intellectual soul as comprehending universals, has a power extending to the infinite; therefore, it cannot be limited by nature to certain fixed natural notions, or even to certain fixed means whether of defense or of clothing, as is the case with other animals, the souls of which are endowed with knowledge and power in regard to fixed and particular things.[18]

To be sure, certain human beings can be compelled by circumstances to remain at the level of animals, concerned exclusively with the necessities of life, but Thomas' point is that this forced restriction of the mind is a sort of denial of the human soul and its limitless aspirations.

In the striking phrase of the twentieth-century Thomist Bernard Lonergan, the mind wants to "know everything about everything."[19] Its object, the food after which it hungers, the drink that alone can satisfy it, is Being itself, the totality of the real, everything about everything.

As our intellect is infinite in power, so does it know the infinite. For its power is indeed infinite inasmuch as it is not terminated by corporeal matter.[20]

It is said in *The Soul* that the soul is, "in some manner, all things," since its nature is such that it can know all things.[21]

We have just seen in the preceding section how passionately Thomas insists on the coming together of soul and body, but here we see the balancing passion for the freedom and expansiveness of the mind. Precisely as immaterial, the human spirit is not tied to the worldly, the particular, the matter-of-fact. Not exclusively sensate, the spirit, as the word itself suggests (*spiritus*), is able to breathe, to fly, to wing its way to the far reaches of whatever is. It is a kind of mirror of being, the clear glass in which all that is can be reflected.

At this point, it is most important to recall Thomas' understanding of God. As became clear in chapter 2, God for Aquinas is not one being among many, not the supreme being, but the ground of the real, *ipsum esse subsistens,* the sheer act of existing. As such, God is the root and source of all of creation, the font from which finite being continually flows. Therefore, to say that the human mind is oriented to the whole of reality is for Thomas simply to say that it is oriented to God, toward that fullness of being that undergirds, suffuses, and infinitely

---

18. *Summa theologiae* 1.76.5 ad 4. Cf. *Summa theologiae* 1.86.2: "Never does our intellect understand so many things, that it cannot understand more."

19. Bernard Lonergan, *Insight: A Study of Human Understanding* (New York: Philosophical Library, 1958), 350–351.

20. *Summa theologiae* 1.86.2 ad. 4.

21. Thomas Aquinas, *Disputed Questions on Truth* 2.2.

surpasses all things. This openness of the spirit to the divine is the "royal dignity," the glory of the human, that which makes us, in a word, the *imago Dei*:

> The image of God is in man . . . first, inasmuch as man possesses a natural aptitude for understanding and loving God; and this aptitude consists in the very nature of the mind, which is common to all men.[22]

We are the reflections of God inasmuch as we are the clear pools in which God's reality can be mirrored. Thomas' point is that we are "built for" union with the divine, marked as it were with the stamp of God's being. And as we've come to expect, this clarification is not merely of theoretical interest. In fact, one could say that the whole of Aquinas' theology and spirituality rests upon this insight. Because we are "predestined," branded with the mark of God, we *are nothing but hunger and thirst for the divine life*. Every energy, every power, every thought and action of ours is, explicitly or implicitly, animated by the divine power, drawn by it and determined by it.

Steven Spielberg has hinted at this classically Christian idea of the *imago Dei* in his film *Close Encounters of the Third Kind*. In time-honored style, Spielberg chooses what lies just beyond the frontier of the known—in this case, UFOs and extraterrestrials—to symbolize and evoke the numinous dimension of God. Early in the film, alien spacecraft appear over a peaceful Midwest town on a summer night. The townspeople who see these unexpected visions are at the same time frightened and fascinated, repelled and irresistibly attracted. Their response suggests, of course, the religious attitude described by Rudolf Otto: in the presence of the divine, one is simultaneously overawed and captivated.[23] Several of the witnesses are marked, "branded," by the blazing light of the spacecraft, and they carry on their bodies afterward a sort of sunburn. This mark penetrates beyond the level of the skin and sears their hearts and minds. They feel compelled, in an obsessive way, to seek out the mountain where the alien mother ship will descend and establish contact with the earth. Overcoming the objections of family and friends, withstanding numerous attacks and surmounting impossible obstacles, two of these witnesses make it to the mountaintop for the ecstatic encounter with the extraterrestrials.

There are obviously numerous religious symbols employed in this film; in fact, it could be read as a compendium of the spiritual life, detailing the movement from conversion through repentance to union. But I want simply to focus on

---

22. *Summa theologiae* 1.93.4.
23. Rudolf Otto, *The Idea of the Holy: An Inquiry into the Non-Rational Factor in the Idea of the Divine and its Relation to the Rational*, 2nd ed., trans. John W. Harvey (Oxford: Oxford University Press, 1950).

the symbol of the brand, the mark, as an evocation of the *imago Dei*. Once they were touched by the supernatural power of the spacecraft, the witnesses' lives were transformed: they were unable to focus on anything but reunion with the ones who had marked them. It was as though the aliens had planted a magnet in them that was then ineluctably drawn to the great magnet of the mountain of encounter. This mark, this inner compulsion, this "magnet," is something like the image of God in us. Whether we are saints or sinners, whether we seek fame or wealth or spiritual wisdom, whether we live responsibly or irresponsibly, *we are inevitably drawn to God* as to our final end. The mountain of encounter, union with the divine, is written into our souls; there is, if you will, a picture, an icon, of this "place" in our hearts, and we follow it whether we want to or not.

> The image of God abides ever in the soul, *whether this image be so obsolete*, as it were clouded, *as to amount to nothing . . . or obscured and disfigured*, as in sinners; or *clear and beautiful* as in the just.[24]

The restlessness of the human being as she makes her way through life is a function of this *imago*, this predestination. We are never satisfied with anything less than the encounter, the union. Even if we have achieved all that one can reasonably desire, we want more because there is this fascinating, annoying, compelling hunger in us for the divine.

What becomes clear too in the above-cited text is the marvelously Catholic confidence that the *imago* can never be totally lost, despite the most blinding ignorance and the most debilitating sin. Even in the worst condition, there is still reason to hope, precisely because of the unbreakable bond between Creator and creature. In some of his more extreme texts, Martin Luther suggests that the *imago Dei* had been destroyed by sin and that as a consequence there is no continuity between the divine and the human.[25] Thomas never adopts such a radical position. For him, sin and stupidity can *obscure*, can *darken* the image, but they can never shatter it. The *imago* is the beautiful jewel that, even when spattered with mud, catches and reflects back some of the divine light. It is that fundamental goodness that can never be totally perverted; it is that wholesome hunger that can lead us finally to the bread of life.

At this point, we ought to be hearing the overtones of a theme that has been sounded frequently in this book. In affirming the presence of the *imago*

---

24. *Summa theologiae* 1.93.8 ad. 3.

25. See, for instance, Martin Luther, *Commentary on Genesis*, vol. 2, trans. John Nicholas Lenker (Minneapolis, MN: Luther, 1910), 95: "If man, having been created both 'in the image' and 'in the likeness' of God, had not fallen, he would have lived forever. . . . But by sin both this 'likeness' and this 'image' were lost."

in all people, even in sinners, Thomas is subtly turning back a negative spiritual attitude. As we have seen before, one of the ruses of the sinner is to claim independence from God in sin itself. In the darkness, self-absorption, and despair of his sinful soul, he can find refuge from the awful press of God. We can hear the cry of such a sinner in Francis Thompson's classic poem:

> I fled Him, down the nights and down the days;
> I fled Him, down the arches of the years;
> I fled Him, down the labyrinthine ways
>   Of my own mind; and in the midst of tears
> I hid from him.[26]

This is the sinner who wants to sever any tie, loosen any bond, unravel any connection to God, someone whose entire life becomes an elaborate attempt to *flee*. Through time and space he runs, and most devastatingly, in the darkness of his mind, he conceals himself, wanting to hide from the face of God. This is a portrait in miniature of someone who purposely attempts to shatter the *imago Dei* because he finds its "weight" too much to bear. But in the spirit of Thomas Aquinas, Francis Thompson reminds us that there is no escape from "those strong Feet that followed, followed after." The "Hound of Heaven" is not so easily put off the trail:

> But with unhurrying chase,
> And unperturbèd pace,
> Deliberate speed, majestic instancy,
>   They beat—and a Voice beat
>   More instant than the Feet —
> "All things betray thee, who betrayest me."[27]

Even as the sinner retreats into the encircling forest gloom of his rebellion, his *imago* gives him away, guiding the divine bloodhound on his hunt. Try as he might to cover it, to put it out, to quench it, the sinner cannot darken the light of the *imago Dei* that shines out from his own heart, beckoning to the searching God.

Another route of escape that Thomas' doctrine of the *imago* cuts off is that of a false or misguided humility. Eager to be free of the divine press, one might claim that she is unworthy of God, incapable of imaging or reflecting God in any

---

26. Francis Thompson, "The Hound of Heaven," in *Selected Poems of Francis Thompson*, 2nd ed. (London: Burns & Oates, 1908), 51.

27. Thompson, 51.

way. To this person Thomas urges a frank acceptance of her royal dignity as a child of God. This doctrine of the *imago* teaches that our basic relationship to the divine is not that of sinner to savior (though that is certainly a dimension of our rapport with God), but rather that of child to parent. At the depths of our being, we are a reflection of the divine beauty, the divine power, the divine mind. There is a "divinity" within us that seeks full expression and full union. This intrinsic holiness of the person is expressed in the Hindu tradition in the greeting gesture of the joined palms, signaling that one is saluting the divinity in the other. It is also implicit in the curious Austrian and South German salutation, "*Grüß Gott,*" which means literally "greeting to God." When one says "*Grüß Gott*" to a friend, he hails the divine spark in that person. Thomas Aquinas, the spiritual master, clearly sees this hidden divinity and compels his reader to see it, to accept it, to come to terms with it.

Perhaps the greatest danger that Thomas highlights in these texts on the *imago* is a sort of forgetfulness of soul, losing sight—through sin or ignorance or indifference—of who we are in our depths. And it is especially here that I see the tremendous relevance of these texts for our time. There is a rebirth of interest today in the ancient category of soul. *Care of the Soul*, a book dealing with the cultivation of one's spirituality, sat atop the *New York Times* bestseller list for several weeks, and a recording of Gregorian chants sung by an obscure group of Spanish monks rocketed up the Billboard charts.[28] These phenomena speak to me of a hunger for the things of the soul after too long a dominance by the rational, the pragmatic, the practical. We are made by God and are therefore built for God. When these facts are forgotten in our technological, economically driven society, the national soul dries up, withers through lack of use. Toward the end of his life, C.G. Jung composed a beautiful meditative book entitled *Modern Man in Search of a Soul.*[29] In this text he witnesses to the growing spiritual aridity of our time, and he argues that a Third World War can be avoided only if human beings begin to cultivate in a systematic way the mysterious divine ground that is the source and center of who they are. Aquinas' writings on the human person are extremely "soulful," reminding us of our dignity and destiny as children of the divine. And as such, they are enormously helpful especially to us pragmatic,

---

28. Thomas Moore, *Care of the Soul: A Guide for Cultivating Depth and Sacredness in Everyday Life* (New York: HarperCollins, 1994). On the astonishing popularity of *Chant*, an album of Gregorian chants by the Benedictine Monks of Santo Domingo de Silos, see Kory Grow, "Flashback: Spanish Monks Ignite Gregorian 'Chant'-Mania," *Rolling Stone*, March 15, 2019, https://www.rollingstone.com/music/music-features/gregorian-chant-album-monks-808107/.

29. Carl Jung, *Modern Man in Search of a Soul*, trans. W.S. Dell and Cary F. Baynes (New York: Harcourt, 1933).

commonsensical Americans. Let us follow this soulful path as we look at his texts dealing with the ultimate happiness of the human being.

The "End" That Is God

It is one of the common beliefs of the great atheists of modern times that the human being is rendered less than human by the belief in God. For the little-known but enormously influential atheist Ludwig Feuerbach, God is a projection of our idealized self-image. According to this nineteenth-century German philosopher, we take whatever we want to be—all-knowing, all-loving, all-powerful—and we project it outward in the form of an imaginary supreme being. Then, in a sort of neurotic reversal, we beg that reality (through prayer) to give us back some of what we have given to it. The result of this unfortunate inner game is that we do not realize ourselves as we should. Lost in contemplation of and reverence for our own imaginary construction, we never seek to *make ourselves* more intelligent, more compassionate, more powerful. Religion, for Feuerbach, becomes therefore the great halter of progress, the negation of authentic humanity.[30]

Feuerbach's theory was to have a decisive impact on his younger contemporary Karl Marx, who argued that belief in God is an "opium of the people."[31] Marx meant, of course, that the fantasy of God and eternal life dulls our sensitivity to our concrete economic and political suffering in the here and now and thus prevents us from making real improvements in our lives. Religion functions as a sort of drug and, like all narcotics, it produces a distorted view of the world and results in irresponsible behavior. For Marx, the irresponsible behavior that flows from religion is just this indifference to improving the lot of alienated and exploited victims of the capitalist system. Once more, the belief in God diminishes us.

A twentieth-century disciple of Ludwig Feuerbach was the founder of psychoanalysis, Sigmund Freud. Like his nineteenth-century forebear, Freud thought that religion is a kind of projection, but he specified the nature of this projection in terms of psychoanalytic theory. For Freud, the belief in God is

30. Ludwig Feuerbach, *The Essence of Christianity*, trans. Mary Ann Evans (New York: Harper & Row, 1957).
31. Karl Marx, "A Contribution to the Critique of Hegel's *Philosophy of Right*: Introduction," in *Critique of Hegel's "Philosophy of Right,"* trans. Annette Jolin and Joseph O'Malley (Cambridge: Cambridge University Press, 1970), 131.

a childish, wish-fulfilling fantasy, an imaginary realization of our deepest and most powerful desires.[32] We want so intensely to live forever, to see justice triumph over injustice, to find meaning in the midst of a meaningless world, that we fantasize—and then project outward—the existence of a super reality who will make these wishes come true. Religion is thus like a waking dream, a fantastic realization of what we *want* but, in fact, cannot realize. As was the case with Feuerbach and Marx, so for Freud this belief is not a harmless mistake, an innocent indulgence; on the contrary, it stands in the way of progress. As long as we remain religious, says Sigmund Freud, we rest at a primitive, childish level of psychological development, never fully embracing freedom, never assuming responsibility, never developing a critical intelligence—and thus never really coming to maturity.

What these three atheists have in common is the conviction that the more God is affirmed, the less we human beings become; the more God is emphasized, the more we are diminished. They assume, in short, what I have called a competitive relationship between God and the world, a zero-sum game in which one partner grows at the expense of the other. Filled with a proper zeal for the betterment of humanity, these thinkers all feel obliged to dispense with the chief competitor to our progress, God. This general atheist perspective is given its most pointed expression in an argument for the nonexistence of God formulated by Jean-Paul Sartre: if God exists, I cannot be free; but I am free; therefore, God does not exist.[33] If there is a supreme being who controls the universe and human affairs, who dominates the universe, who competes with us, then there can be no real freedom. Thus, the fact of our freedom and dignity effectively moves God off the stage.

The only proper answer to these atheists, in my view, is to affirm, as I have at various points in this book, the *noncompetitive relationship between God and the world*. Because God is not a supreme being, but rather Being itself, God does not enter into a rapport of rivalry with the universe or with any creature in it. As the ground of being, the deepest source of the universe's existence, God is that power in which we find our authentic freedom, in whom we can be most ourselves. Therefore, we do not have to eradicate God in order to be ourselves completely; on the contrary. It is in surrendering to the alluring call of the divine that we are most free, most ourselves, most at home. It is this understanding of the God-world relationship that inspires Thomas' extraordinarily rich analysis of the "final

---

32. Sigmund Freud, *The Future of an Illusion*, trans. Gregory C. Richter, ed. Todd Dufresne (Toronto: Broadview, 2012), 92–95, 98–100.

33. See Jean-Paul Sartre, *Existentialism Is a Humanism*, trans. Carol Macomber, ed. John Kulka (New Haven, CT: Yale University Press, 2007), 28–29.

end" or ultimate happiness of the human being: we come home to ourselves only in embarking on the fascinating journey outward to God.

In a Buddhist perspective, desire is the chief spiritual problem. Precisely inasmuch as we cling to our desires, say the Buddhists, we remain caught in the realm of illusion and suffering. When we let go of desire, blowing out the candle of egotistic craving, we discover that *nirvana* which is the "goal" of the spiritual life. Like most of his Christian forebears, Thomas Aquinas proposes a different way, a spiritual path that begins and ends with desire.

Whenever a human being acts, she acts with a particular end or purpose in mind. Thus, the reader of this book is perusing its pages, presumably, to learn something about Thomas Aquinas or about the spiritual life. Now, if we continue to analyze a given act, to ask ever-more-penetrating questions about it, we see that its intentional range opens up remarkably. Thus, you might be reading this book in order to learn something about Aquinas' thought so that you can be better prepared for a course on Aquinas that you will be taking next fall, so that you can fulfill one of the requirements for a master's degree, so that eventually you might be in a position to pursue a doctorate, so that someday you might become a university professor, so that you can pass on the wisdom of the spiritual tradition in a profound way, so that you can move other people into more intimate communion with God, so that thereby you can fulfill the deepest sense of vocation that you have, so that, in an ultimate sense, you might be happy. With regard to any act that we perform, says Thomas, we could do a similar analysis, opening up the ever-greater context of desire in which that act is situated. In any case, he claims, we come in the end to a final or ultimate goal that, whether we are explicitly aware of it or not, is determining what we do. This is, as I suggested above, nothing but the desire to be happy, to be finally satisfied, to be at peace. Without this basic craving of the heart, we would never do anything:

> If there were no last end, nothing would be desired, nor would any action have its term, nor would the intention of the agent be at rest; while if there is no first thing among those that are ordained to the end, none would begin to work at anything.[34]

Just as there must be a first mover with regard to physical change in the universe, so must there be a first mover of the will, an uncaused cause of the movement of the heart, and this is none other than the desire for perfect contentment. Even someone who commits suicide does so, in an admittedly twisted way, out

---

34. *Summa theologiae* 1-2.1.4.

of a desire for happiness. Again, most of us are entirely unaware of this deep conditioning of the will as we go about our daily business. But whether we are tossing a baseball, listening to a lecture, mindlessly watching a television program, or idly whistling to ourselves, we are, indirectly at least, desiring our ultimate fulfillment.

What Thomas expresses in philosophical language is something that is reflected in the mythological literature of the world: the sacred quest. Transhistorically and transculturally one can see in drama, liturgy, poetry, and dance this theme of the journey, the search for the ever-elusive prize that alone will make life meaningful. Less than a century before Aquinas wrote, there appeared in the West the first versions of the Grail legend, composed by Chretien de Troyes and Robert de Boron. In these first tellings of the tale, the Grail, the cup that Christ used at the Last Supper and that caught some of his blood as it poured from his side, is in the possession of the Fisher King, a man who bears a mysteriously incurable wound. As long as he suffers, the country that he rules languishes. Only if a naïve and innocent man finds the Grail—and has the temerity to ask about its meaning and purpose—will the Fisher King be healed and the fortunes of his country revived. Early in the story, the knight, Perceval, stumbles upon the castle of the king and sees the Grail carried in a magnificent procession, but he is too stunned or too intimidated to ask the meaning of this mysterious object. Accordingly, he is expelled from the castle and the king remains wounded. The rest of the story is the account of Perceval's adventurous quest for the Holy Grail, his attempt to rediscover the castle of the wounded king and to bring healing to him and his nation.

The Grail effectively symbolizes what Aquinas calls the "last end," that goal that animates the journey of one's life and that alone can satisfy and bring healing to the soul. For Thomas, and for the authors of the Grail legends, human life is basically an endeavor, a quest, a gradual opening out of will and consciousness. As Perceval makes his way through five painful years of searching for the Grail, he gradually discovers the true significance of this object that has become his obsession. Similarly, for Thomas Aquinas, the human heart and mind expand as they push outward toward the happiness that they crave. It is only in the course of the adventure that is human striving that a person comes fully to understand and appreciate that mysterious reality that alone can satisfy. Along the way, he tends to settle on goals or ends that are not ultimate, and it is his very dissatisfaction that spurs him on toward his proper fulfillment. Much of the energy and dynamism of the spiritual life for Aquinas flows from this sometimes satisfying, often disappointing, frequently confusing, and always dramatic quest for the Holy Grail of joy.

Having determined that all people are questing for ultimate contentment, Aquinas next endeavors to search out the nature of this happiness and to discover the process by which it can be obtained. In the course of this analysis, he considers most of the holy grails that have been sought by human beings over the centuries, and he shows how they fall short in various ways of the true Grail. What he shows most fundamentally are the myriad paths by which one's "soul," one's deepest center and source of life, can be lost.

First he wonders whether our ultimate happiness consists in the possession of wealth—as many seem to have thought over the ages.[35] There are, he says, two types of wealth: natural and artificial. Natural wealth is that which satisfies the basic desires of the human body: food, clothing, transportation, shelter, and the like; whereas artificial wealth, or money, is that which is invented by human beings in order to facilitate exchange. Now, natural wealth cannot be the final end because it exists for something greater—namely, the overall "support of human nature."[36] What Thomas means here is that food, shelter, clothing, and transportation are means to the end of general bodily contentment; they are meant not to be enjoyed for their own sake, but rather to give rise to a sense of satisfaction and peace. Thus, they cannot, in themselves, be what human beings ultimately desire. With regard to artificial wealth—money, stocks, bonds, investments, etc.—we are even further from the ultimate goal of one's life because such things are used only for the procurement of natural wealth, only to buy those objects that give us bodily satisfaction. In neither case, concludes Aquinas, do we finally rest in our material possessions. Instead we treasure them as values subordinated to higher ends. If we were to prize our wealth as the highest good, we would be, says Thomas, in the grip of a sort of spiritual—we might say psychological—illness. We would be overwhelmed by what the medievals called "concupiscence" or misguided desire.

This pithy analysis of wealth, drawn largely from Aristotle, has a remarkably contemporary resonance. We live in a culture that is dominated by the concupiscent desire for what Thomas calls natural and artificial wealth. Joseph Campbell, the mythologist, has observed that in the Middle Ages the tallest building in a town would be the church, since spiritual values were seen as self-evidently the most important; in the Renaissance, the government headquarters came to dominate the city since the "ultimate concern" of the community had begun to shift to the affairs of this-worldly power. Today, continues Campbell, even a casual glance at one of our great cities reveals that a third shift has occurred.

---

35. *Summa theologiae* 1-2.2.1.
36. *Summa theologiae* 1-2.2.1.

If one surveys the skylines of downtown New York or Chicago, one is hard-pressed to notice any church steeples.[37] Indeed, even the bishops' cathedrals, the foci of spiritual activity, St. Patrick's and Holy Name, are tucked away, lost in the shadows of the towering secular buildings that dwarf them. And the mayors' offices in those two cities—the centers of political power—are also relatively inconspicuous. But what cannot be missed, what brood over the cities like sentinels, what block out the sun and obscure the night sky are the mighty temples of business and wealth: the Empire State Building, the Willis Tower, the Standard Oil Building. If, as Ruskin indicated, we can sense the ethos of a people most clearly in the "book of their art," in what they concretely produce, then there is no doubt that we as a society are under the sway of wealth.[38] In fact, "the American dream," now exported around the globe, is tantamount to material success, to the amassing of possessions, and its influence can be seen in ubiquitous advertising and in the excesses of popular culture. To have more and more, to be richer and richer, to guarantee our security through "things" is, I would submit, a sort of American original sin—and a poison that has spread well beyond the confines of our borders.

In his simple arguments, St. Thomas Aquinas reminds us that this sort of concupiscent desire for wealth is soul-destroying, since it aligns our properly infinite hunger for joy with an object that can never satisfy that hunger:

> For when we already possess them [material goods] we despise them, and seek others: which is the sense of Our Lord's words: "Whosoever drinketh of this water," by which temporal goods are signified, "shall thirst again." The reason of this is that we realize more their insufficiency when we possess them: and this very fact shows that they are imperfect and that the sovereign good does not consist therein.[39]

Paul Tillich commented that concupiscence is the "attempt to cram the whole world into one's mouth,"[40] futilely trying to satisfy the thirst for God with something less than divine. This very psychological/spiritual problem, implies Tillich, leads to the addictive behavior so typical of our time. Whether someone is addicted to wealth, power, pleasure, or drugs, one circles obsessively around a finite object, trying again and again to fill up the unlimited emptiness he

---

37. Joseph Campbell with Bill Moyers, *The Power of Myth*, ed. Betty Sue Flowers (New York: Anchor Books, 1991), 118–119.

38. John Ruskin, *St. Mark's Rest: The History of Venice*, 2nd ed. (London: George Allen, 1894), vii.

39. *Summa theologiae* 1-2.2.1 ad. 3.

40. Quoted in Langdon Gilkey, *Gilkey on Tillich* (Eugene, OR: Wipf and Stock, 2000), 129.

feels within. This addictive style is beautifully symbolized in the story that Thomas invokes in the above example—namely, that of the woman at the well: "whosoever drinketh of this water will thirst again." Thomas is searching for that "object" that alone can finally satisfy the thirst of the soul.

Having excluded wealth as this final end, he next considers honors, fame, and glory.[41] Some people are relatively uninterested in material goods, preferring above all the good opinion of others, the glory that shines on them because of their accomplishments and virtues. In a certain sense, this choice of a final end represents a greater refinement of spirit than the option for material wealth, presupposing a dedication to great ideals and a willingness to sacrifice one's self-interest. But Thomas reveals the subtle spiritual dangers involved in identifying this value with the highest good. First, he says, honor is given to someone in recognition of a virtue, achievement, or goodness, and it is thus a sign or symbol, an indicator of perfection—and not itself a perfection. Therefore, it can in no sense be identified with the final end of a human being. What Thomas underscores here, in a word, is ambition:

> Virtue's true reward is happiness itself, for which the virtuous work; whereas if they worked for honor, it would no longer be virtue but ambition.[42]

When the fleeting sign of goodness is sought as a good in itself, we see another peculiar skewing of ultimate concern, another sort of psychological/spiritual disorder.

Similarly, fame and glory, which consist, as Ambrose says, in being well-known and praised, cannot be themselves the ultimate joy of a human being because they are so fleeting, so insubstantial, and so often mistaken:

> We must observe that human knowledge often fails, especially in contingent singulars, such as are human acts. For this reason, human glory is frequently deceptive.[43]

One could be famous and highly thought of—but for all the wrong reasons. As is obvious in our experience, it is frequently those people who exhibit the fewest virtues who are the most vociferously praised and widely celebrated. We know how often people are impressed by the stupid, the vulgar, the simplistic, and the sensuously pleasurable but unmoved by authentic virtue, truth, and beauty.

---

41. *Summa theologiae* 1-2.2.2–3.
42. *Summa theologiae* 1-2.2.2 ad. 1.
43. *Summa theologiae* 1-2.2.3.

Thus, it is altogether possible—indeed likely—that fame and esteem are counter-indications of one's real goodness.

Once more, I think that these observations of Aquinas are of some relevance to our time in which celebrity itself sometimes seems to be the ultimate concern. Rock stars, movie actors, singers, athletes, politicians, even criminals—the various gods proposed by the popular culture—emerge as models to be emulated. Certain television shows celebrate celebrity itself, as if being well-known—having one's fifteen minutes of fame as Andy Warhol archly predicted for all of us—was itself worthy of our attention.

But it is just this sort of obsession with glitter and glamor—what Thomas calls glory—that leads to a loss of soul. It is obvious to anyone with any life experience that the stars of today are, with rare exceptions, forgotten tomorrow. As Paul Simon says in his song "The Boy in the Bubble," "every generation throws a hero up the pop charts." Celebrities come and go, buoyed up by the fleeting bubble of public opinion, tossed about on the wave of "glory." And, to be sure, this phenomenon is not restricted to the world of entertainment and popular culture. As Thomas himself seems to indicate, the lust for glory is manifested in ambitions of all kinds, the desire not to serve but to be admired for one's prominence. This soul-sickness can creep into the hearts of politicians, lawyers, business executives, academics, and priests. When seeking after this ephemeral goal, one finds oneself on what the medievals called "the wheel of fortune," the ever-rotating circle of *fortuna,* luck, prominence, public adulation. One can be on the top, but one's stay there is necessarily short, since the wheel inexorably turns. In time, one is inevitably on the bottom, cursing one's fate and longing for the next moment in the sun. On this wheel of glory, a person is like the sinners in the first circle of Dante's Inferno, turning and turning, buffeted by the winds of desire and lust, chasing first this banner then that, but making no progress and finding no anchor. The point is to stand not on the outside of the wheel, on the ever-rotating rim, but rather to find one's anchor in the center, that still point that remains the same despite all change. This deepest center, this quiet place of rest and stability, that divine ground which we discover in prayer, is what Thomas is searching for in this analysis of the final end.

If neither material wealth nor the admiration of others qualifies as the Holy Grail, then perhaps the hedonists are right in saying that bodily pleasure is the joy that we all ultimately seek. Indeed Thomas admits that pleasure seems to be something pursued purely for its own sake; no one wonders why we want to experience bodily pleasure. Yet he insists at the same time that the pleasure sensed by the body is but a "trifle as compared with the good of the soul." In order to understand what he means here we have to recall that the soul is that capacity of ours to be open to the fullness of reality, that dynamism that pushes us out to know everything about everything, to contemplate Being itself. It is our *capacitas universi,* our capacity for the universe. But the bodily senses are oriented toward the particular, toward this sight, this sound, this experience. Their range, in short, is far more restricted than that of the soul. Therefore, the ultimate good, the final joy, of human life, that which satisfies the broadest and deepest of our desires, cannot be something as restricted as a bodily pleasure, but must on the contrary be an infinite value appreciated by the soul:

> Consequently it is evident that that good which is fitting to the body, and which causes bodily delight . . . is not man's perfect good, but is quite a trifle as compared with the good of the soul.[44]

Once more, Thomas Aquinas is inviting us to ecstasy. Were we convinced that our ultimate good consists in pleasure, we would never leave the confines of our own bodies, never transcend the basic joys associated with satisfying biological needs for food and sex and comfort. But as Thomas continually insists, we were built for more than that; we were built for the universe, for a constant leap of self-transcendence in love. Placing bodily pleasure at the center of one's life is the quickest route to what Paul Tillich calls "self-complacent finitude," the self-satisfied, spiritually lazy attitude of resting in oneself. Thomas' anthropology assumes that there is a restlessness in all of us, an inner goad, a gadfly of the heart, that spurs us on to a vision of the fullness of reality. An orientation to pleasure above all things is a putting out of that inner fire, a surrender to spiritual torpor and sloth. Now, as should be clear from an earlier section of this chapter, Thomas has no quarrel with the body and indeed remains convinced that bodily pleasure *accompanies* even the vision of God, but he is equally convinced that the placing of pleasure at the center of one's life is tantamount to spiritual suicide.

How often it happens that someone who has spent the first half of his life in a single-minded pursuit of pleasure finds that a bottoming out occurs at midlife. As he makes the transition to the second half of life, he finds himself in a wasteland, a desert of depression, anxiety, and fear. The objects and activities that he used to savor now leave him flat and deeply unsatisfied. I cannot help but observe that this dryness of soul is remarkably typical of many in our culture today. Sated with every pleasure imaginable, many people remain stubbornly unfulfilled. In the language of Jungian psychology, such people are shifting from the narrow concerns of the ego to the deeper and broader spiritual concerns of the Self. They are painfully opening out in the realization that the soul is hungrier than

---

44. *Summa theologiae* 1-2.2.6.

they had imagined, that they have a destiny beyond the narrow limitations of bodily satisfaction. For the Jungians, this midlife desert experience is of decisive spiritual significance and power, for it is the only way that one's psyche is jarred into deeper life and vision.

I would argue that Thomas Aquinas makes a very similar case. His diagnosis of the spiritual illness of so many in our pleasure-oriented society would be "shrinking of soul," a narrowing down to the particular, the egocentric. And his recommendation would be to burst the self-imposed boundaries of the soul and fly outside of oneself on the sheer energy of one's desire for the ultimate. He wants us to lift up our eyes "to the mountains" from whence comes our help (Ps. 121:1), to open wide the vision of the spirit to broader horizons.

Not wealth, not glory, not bodily pleasure, the final joy of the human being must be that which "lulls the appetite altogether," that which satisfies every longing, that which corresponds to the infinite craving of the human heart.

> Now the object of the will, i.e., of man's appetite, is the universal good. . . .
> Hence it is evident that nothing can lull the human will but the universal
> good. This is to be found, not in any creature, but in God alone; because every
> creature has goodness by participation. Thus God alone can satisfy the will of
> man.[45]

With this pithy comment, Thomas has found the Holy Grail. Because we are "wired" for God from the beginning, God alone is the end of human life. Only when we leap out of ourselves in a radical embrace of the fullness of reality will our desire be quenched; only when we hook our unlimited longing to an unlimited good will we find the joy for which we were created. Nothing less than everything, than Being itself, than the divine energy will fill up the emptiness of the human heart. Nothing other than a concrete and complete imitation of Christ, the ecstatic lover of God, will bring us to life.

Does this mean that we must eschew any good other than God, that we must turn radically away from wealth and pleasure and practical achievement, embracing the life of a contemplative monk? By no means. But we must place the love of God at the center of all, making it the ground and reason for everything else that we do. Just as God does not compete with the world, so the love of God is not in competition with other ends and goods and goals. Once the divine center is clearly established in one's life, one can, as Augustine implied, do as one wills, singing, playing, relating, trading, entering into relationships—all for the glory of God.

---

45. *Summa theologiae* 1-2.2.8.

The Holy Grail is what Thomas Aquinas calls the "beatific vision," the sight, or rather the experience, of God. Can we have this vision in this life? Yes, says Thomas, when we accept the divine power as the goal and focus of our lives, when we give ourselves to God in prayer, when we lose ourselves in love and contemplation, we are experiencing—in a vague and anticipatory fashion—the beatific vision. In this sense, we can be happy, joy-filled, in this life. No gloomy pessimist, Thomas is convinced that we were created for happiness, for the imitation of the divine joy. At the same time, he holds that absolute happiness, full vision of the divine reality, is reserved for the life that comes beyond this one, when our receptive capacities are expanded through the gift of God's grace. This last observation is of decisive significance. Since the fullness of joy lies beyond the range and scope of this life, we will always be restless this side of death. Since the beatific vision is completely had only in the life to come, we will never be fully satisfied, finally content, totally at rest in this life. Rather, all of one's earthly existence is characterized, appropriately, by a hunger, a longing, a push outward and upward, a stubborn dissatisfaction. And therefore no utopia—of a political, economic, or psychological kind—should ever be expected. No program, no restructuring of institutions, no revolution, and no personal reorientation will ever result in human bliss; in biblical language, no Tower of Babel will ever reach up to God. But, as I suggested above, this should not frustrate us; rather, it should spur us on. When he was a young man, G.K. Chesterton was convinced that ultimate happiness could be had in this life—and thus he found himself in a constant state of disappointment because that happiness refused to materialize.

It was only, he said, when he became a Christian and realized that one was not meant to be fully content in this life that he began to enjoy himself! What changed in Chesterton was the way that he related to the world: once he knew that he didn't have to cling to it in a desperate attempt to derive happiness from it, he relaxed and allowed its simple beauty and joy to enter in.

Conclusion

Once more it all comes down to ecstasy. God, who is nothing but love, has planted in the human heart an impulse to love. We are branded, marked, stamped with the image of love, and we are compelled, from our earliest days, by the hunger for love. When we fail to love, we are miserable, and when we enter into love, we are filled with life. We are wired for self-forgetfulness, built for the journey out of ourselves, lured finally by the "love that moves the planets and the stars." All of this is Thomas Aquinas' way of saying that we are "made in the image and likeness of God" and endowed with an immortal soul. The greatest tragedy is not failing to live up to the divine call (who does not fail after all?) but rather forgetting about our destiny altogether, living as if we were not children of God, acting as if we were not hungrily pursued by the hound of heaven. For Thomas Aquinas the greatest tragedy is loss of vision, loss of breadth, loss of divine ecstasy, loss of soul.

And this human drama, this mystical journey into the divine, does not take place in some rarefied spiritual realm, cut off from earth, from color and relationship and sight and sound. Rather, it is an adventure of the entire person, of the embodied soul and the ensouled body, of the incarnate spirit that, in its strange beauty, uniquely mirrors something of God's being. God created us the way he did—flesh and spirit—because, like an artist, he loves wonderful hybrids, and he invites us to come even to the innermost courts of heaven clothed still in the body he gave us. To bring the grubby flesh right into the heart of the beatific vision is one of Aquinas' humanist masterstrokes.

Enfleshed, built for ecstasy, destined for a deifying beatific vision, we are all in the image of Jesus Christ. Thomas' "theological anthropology" can be summed up in the phrase, "to live in Christ Jesus." To live in the self-forgetting and self-transcending love of God, to allow the divine and human to meet and mingle in one's very flesh, to open the eyes of the soul to the vision of God is to live *in Christo*. It is, in a word, to be a disciple.

CONCLUSION

A ll of Christian theology and spirituality centers around a few basic questions: Who are we? Who or what is God? How do we and God come together? As I have suggested throughout this book, it is the last of these three questions that is the most fundamental and the most important. For a Christian, the answer to that third question is Jesus the Christ. In him, we see the harmonizing, the soulful embrace, of the aching human spirit and the ecstatic outreach of God. In him, we know who we are in the deepest sense and we realize, to our delight and surprise, just who God is. To put it in the pithy language of the theologians, anthropology and theology are read, for Christians, always in light of Christology.

Throughout this book I have tried to show that Thomas Aquinas, like John of the Cross, like Teresa of Avila, like Meister Eckhart, like Augustine and Origen, like Francis de Sales, like Thomas Merton, is a Christian spiritual master. Like those great doctors of the soul, Thomas is continually luring his reader onto the ground of the Gospel, onto the field of force opened up by Jesus Christ. And as I have continually maintained, for Aquinas this Gospel way of being is characterized by ecstasy. Christians are those people who, electrified by God's leap out of himself in love, realize that, in the words of Thérèse of Lisieux, their vocation is love.[1]

The only proper response to the self-forgetting of the ground of being is our own radical self-forgetting in love. Thus, who is God for Thomas Aquinas? God is that strange and disturbing reality whose love and power and goodness infinitely surpass our puny capacity to understand or our pathetic attempts to control. Who are we? We are those creatures who are—whether we like it or not—tied to this divine storm, this uncontrollable force, this enigma, this abyss. And thus we are those whose lives are fulfilled in surrender and obedience—in the concrete *imitatio Christi*, the imitation of Christ. As Thomas so often repeats,

---

1. See *Story of a Soul: The Autobiography of St. Thérèse of Lisieux*, 3rd ed., trans. John Clarke (Washington, DC: ICS, 1996), 194.

God's being is diffusive of itself, and as he so often implies, our lives are found in laying them down in service of that ecstasy.

For Thomas Aquinas, God's most characteristic act is the jest of the Incarnation, and our appropriate response is sustained and soul-expanding laughter. Everything else is commentary.

SUGGESTED READING

Burrell, David. *Aquinas: God and Action*. London: Routledge, 1979.

Chenu, Marie-Dominique. *Toward Understanding St. Thomas*. Translated by Albert M. Landry. Chicago: H. Regnery, 1964.

Chesterton, G.K. *Saint Thomas Aquinas: "The Dumb Ox."* New York: Image Books, 1956.

Copleston, F.C. *Aquinas: An Introduction to the Life and Work of the Great Medieval Thinker*. Baltimore, MD: Penguin Books, 1955.

Feser, Edward. *Aquinas: A Beginner's Guide*. Oxford: Oneworld, 2009.

Gilson, Etienne. *The Christian Philosophy of St. Thomas Aquinas*. Translated by L.K. Shook. New York: Random House, 1956.

Pieper, Josef. *Guide to Thomas Aquinas*. Translated by Richard and Clara Winston. New York: New American Library, 1964.

Sertillanges, A.G. *St. Thomas Aquinas and His Work*. Translated by Godfrey Anstruther. London: Burns, Oates, and Washbourne, 1933.

BIBLIOGRAPHY

Anselm. *Anselm: Monologion and Proslogion*. Translated by Thomas Williams. Indianapolis, IN: Hackett, 1996.

———. *On Free Will*. Translated by Ralph McInerny. In *Anselm of Canterbury: The Major Works*, edited by Brian Davies and G.R. Evans, 175–192. Oxford: Oxford University Press, 1998.

———. *Why God Became Man*. Translated by Janet Fairweather. In *Anselm of Canterbury: The Major Works*, edited by Brian Davies and G.R. Evans, 260–357. Oxford: Oxford University Press, 1998.

Aristotle. *Nicomachean Ethics*. Translated by David Ross. Oxford: Oxford University Press, 2009.

Augustine. *Confessiones*. In Patrologia cursus completus, series Latina, edited by J.-P. Migne, 32:660–868. Paris, 1845. In English as *Confessions*. Translated by F.J. Sheed. Edited by Michael P. Foley. Park Ridge, IL: Word on Fire Classics, 2017.

———. *Sermones de scripturis* 117: *De verbis Evangelii Joannis 1:1–3*. In Patrologia cursus completus, series Latina, edited by J.-P. Migne, 38:661–671. Paris, 1865. English translation in *The Works of Saint Augustine: A Translation for the 21st Century*, pt. 3, vol. 4, *Essential Sermons*, translated by Edmund Hill, edited by Boniface Ramsey, 195–202. Hyde Park, NY: New City, 2007.

Balthasar, Hans Urs von. *Dare We Hope "That All Men Be Saved"?* 2nd ed. Translated by David Kipp and Lothar Krauth. San Francisco: Ignatius Press, 2014.

———. "Theologians and Saints." In *Explorations in Theology*, vol. 1, *The Word Made Flesh*, translated by A.V. Littledale with Alexander Dru, 181–210. San Francisco: Ignatius Press, 1989.

Barth, Karl. *Church Dogmatics*, vol. 1, *The Doctrine of the Word of God*, pt. 1. Translated by G.W. Bromiley. Edinburgh: T&T Clark, 1975.

———. *The Epistle to the Romans*. Translated by Edwyn Hoskyns. Oxford: Oxford University Press, 1968.

Bernard of Clairvaux. *Sermons on the Song of Songs*. In *Selected Works*, edited by J. Farina, translated by G.R. Evans, 207–278. Mahwah, NJ: Paulist, 1987.

Calvin, John. *A Commentary on the Psalms of David*. Vol. 3. Oxford: Talboys, 1840. https://books.google.com/.

Campbell, Joseph with Bill Moyers. *The Power of Myth*. Edited by Betty Sue Flowers. New York: Anchor Books, 1991.

Chesterton, G.K. *Saint Thomas Aquinas: "The Dumb Ox."* New York: Image Books, 1956.

———. "Tolerating Other Religions." In *The Collected Works of G.K. Chesterton*, vol. 29, *The Illustrated London News: 1911–1913*, edited by Lawrence J. Clipper, 500–503. San Francisco: Ignatius Press, 1990.

Clark, Kenneth. *Civilisation: A Personal View*. New York: Harper & Row, 1969.

Colledge, Edmund. "The Legend of Thomas Aquinas." In *St. Thomas Aquinas 1274–1974*, 1:13–28. Commemorative Studies. Toronto: Pontifical Institute of Mediaeval Studies, 1974.

Davies, Brian. *Thomas Aquinas's Summa Contra Gentiles: A Guide and Commentary*. Oxford: Oxford University Press, 2016.

De Lubac, Henri. *The Mystery of the Supernatural*. Translated by Rosemary Sheed. New York: Herder & Herder, 1967.

Descartes, René. *The Philosophical Writings of Descartes*, vol. 3, *The Correspondence*. Translated by John Cottingham, Robert Stoothoff, Dugland Murdoch, and Anthony Kenny. Cambridge University Press, 1991.

Eckhart, Meister. "German Sermon 52." In *Meister Eckhart: The Essential Sermons, Commentaries, Treatises, and Defense*. Translated by Edmund Colledge and Bernard McGinn. Mahwah, NJ: Paulist, 1981.

Feuerbach, Ludwig. *The Essence of Christianity*. Translated by Mary Ann Evans. New York: Harper & Row, 1957.

Foster, Kenelm, ed. and trans. *The Life of Saint Thomas Aquinas: Biographical Documents*. London: Longmans & Green, 1959.

Francis of Assisi. "The Canticle of Brother Sun." In *Francis and Clare: The Complete Works*, translated by Regis J. Armstrong and Ignatius C. Brady, 37–39. Mahwah, NJ: Paulist, 1982.

Freud, Sigmund. *The Future of an Illusion*. Translated by Gregory C. Richter. Edited by Todd Dufresne. Toronto: Broadview, 2012.

Gilkey, Langdon. *Gilkey on Tillich*. Eugene, OR: Wipf & Stock, 2000.

Greeley, Andrew M. *Sacraments of Love: A Prayer Journal*. New York: Crossroad, 1994.

Grow, Kory. "Flashback: Spanish Monks Ignite Gregorian 'Chant'-Mania." *Rolling Stone*. March 15, 2019. https://www.rollingstone.com/music/music-features/gregorian-chant-album-monks-808107/.

Guillaume de Tocco. *Ystoria sancti Thome de Aquino de Guillaume de Tocco (1323)*. Edited by Claire le Brun-Gouanvic. Toronto: Pontifical Institute of Mediaeval Studies, 1996.

Heidegger, Martin. *Being and Time*. Translated by John Macquarrie and Edward Robinson. New York: Harper Perennial, 2008.

Hopkins, Gerard Manley. "God's Grandeur." In *Ignatian Collection*, edited by Holly Ordway and Daniel Seseske, 179. Park Ridge, IL: Word on Fire Classics, 2020.

Hume, David. *Dialogues Concerning Natural Religion: And Other Writings*. Edited by Dorothy Coleman. Cambridge: Cambridge University Press, 2007.

Joyce, James. *A Portrait of the Artist as a Young Man*. Mineola, NY: Dover, 1994.

Jung, Carl G. *The Jung–White Letters*. Edited by Ann Conrad Lammers and Adrian Cunningham. London: Routledge, 2007.

———. *Modern Man in Search of a Soul*. Translated by W.S. Dell and Cary F. Baynes. New York: Harcourt, 1933.

———. *Psychological Types*. Translated by H.G. Baynes. Revised by R.F.C. Hull. In *The Collected Works of C.G. Jung*, vol. 6. Edited by Herbert Read, Michael Fordham, Gerhard Adler, and William McGuire. Princeton, NJ: Princeton University Press, 1976.

Kerr, Fergus. "Christ in the *Summa Theologiae*." In *After Aquinas: Versions of Thomism*, 162–180. Malden, MA: Blackwell, 2002.

LaCugna, Catherine Mowry. *God for Us: The Trinity and Christian Life*. Chicago: HarperOne, 1973.

Lonergan, Bernard. *Insight: A Study of Human Understanding*. New York: Philosophical Library, 1958.

Louth, Andrew. *The Origins of the Christian Mystical Tradition from Plato to Denys*. Oxford: Clarendon, 1983.

Luther, Martin. *The Babylonian Captivity of the Church*. In *Martin Luther's Basic Theological Writings*, 3rd ed., edited by Timothy F. Lull and William R. Russell, 196–224. Minneapolis, MN: Fortress, 2012.

———. *Commentary on Genesis*, vol. 2. Translated by John Nicholas Lenker. Minneapolis, MN: Luther, 1910.

———. *Disputation against Scholastic Theology*. In *Martin Luther's Basic Theological Writings*, 3rd ed., edited by Timothy F. Lull and William R. Russell, 3–7. Minneapolis, MN: Fortress, 2012.

Marx, Karl. *Critique of Hegel's "Philosophy of Right."* Translated by Annette Jolin and Joseph O'Malley. Cambridge: Cambridge University Press, 1970.

Merton, Thomas. *Contemplative Prayer.* New York: Image Books, 1996.

———. *The Seven Storey Mountain.* Park Ridge, IL: Word on Fire Classics, 2017.

Moore, Thomas. *Care of the Soul: A Guide for Cultivating Depth and Sacredness in Everyday Life.* New York: HarperCollins, 1994.

Murray, Paul. *Aquinas at Prayer: The Bible, Mysticism, and Poetry.* London: Bloomsbury, 2013.

Nicholas of Cusa. *De docta ignorantia.* In *Nicolai de Cusa Opera Omnia*, vol. 1. Edited by Ernestus Hoffman and Raymundus Klibansky. Hamburg: Meiner, 1932. In English as *Nicholas of Cusa on Learned Ignorance: A Translation and Appraisal of* De Docta Ignorantia. 2nd ed. Translated by Jasper Hopkins. Minneapolis, MN: Arthur J. Banning, 1985.

Nutt, Roger. "From Within the Mediation of Christ: The Place of Christ in the Christian Moral and Sacramental Life According to St. Thomas Aquinas." *Nova et Vetera* 5, no. 4 (Fall 2007): 817–841.

Otto, Rudolf. *The Idea of the Holy: An Inquiry into the Non-Rational Factor in the Idea of the Divine and Its Relation to the Rational.* 2nd ed. Translated by John W. Harvey. Oxford: Oxford University Press, 1950.

Pauck, Wilhelm and Marion Pauck. *Paul Tillich: His Life and Thought*, vol. 1: *Life.* New York: Harper & Row, 1976.

Pieper, Josef. *Guide to Thomas Aquinas.* Translated by Richard and Clara Winston. New York: New American Library, 1964.

Plato. *Plato: Complete Works.* Edited by John M. Cooper and D.S. Hutchinson. Indianapolis, IN: Hackett, 1997.

Porphyry. *On the Life of Plotinus and the Arrangement of His Work.* In *Plotinus: The Enneads*, translated by Stephen MacKenna, 2nd ed., revised by B.S. Page, 1–20. London: Faber, 1956.

Pseudo-Dionysius. *The Divine Names.* In *Pseudo-Dionysius: The Complete Works*, translated by Colm Luibheid, 47–131. New York: Paulist, 1987.

Rahner, Karl. "Anonymous and Explicit Faith." In *Theological Investigations*, vol. 16: *Experience of the Spirit: Source of Theology*, translated by David Morland, 52–78. New York: Seabury, 1979.

———. "Current Problems in Christology." In *Theological Investigations*, vol. 1: *God, Christ, Mary and Grace*, translated by Cornelius Ernst, 149–200. Baltimore, MD: Helicon, 1961.

Ruskin, John. *St. Mark's Rest: The History of Venice*. 2nd ed. London: George Allen, 1894.

Sartre, Jean-Paul. *Existentialism Is a Humanism*. Translated by Carol Macomber. Edited by John Kulka. New Haven, CT: Yale University Press, 2007.

Shea, John. "Sharon's Christmas Prayer." In *Seeing Haloes: Christmas Poems to Open the Heart*, 36–38. Collegeville, MN: Liturgical, 2017.

Spezzano, Daria. *The Glory of God's Grace: Deification According to St. Thomas Aquinas*. Ave Maria, FL: Sapientia, 2015.

Teilhard de Chardin, Pierre. *The Divine Milieu*. Rev. ed. Edited by Bernard Wall. Translated by Bernard Wall et al. New York: Harper Perennial, 2001.

———. *The Phenomenon of Man*. Translated by Bernard Wall. New York: Harper Perennial, 1959.

———. *Writings in Time of War*. Translated by René Hague. London: Collins, 1968.

Thérèse of Lisieux. *Story of a Soul: The Autobiography of St. Thérèse of Lisieux*. 3rd ed. Translated by John Clarke. Washington, DC: ICS, 1996.

Thomas Aquinas. *The Apostles' Creed*. In *The Three Greatest Prayers: Commentaries on the Lord's Prayer, the Hail Mary, and the Apostles' Creed*, translated by Laurence Shapcote, 3–96. Manchester, NH: Sophia Institute, 1990.

———. *Commentary on Dionysius' On the Divine Names*. Translated by Urban Hannon. Latin/English Edition of the Works of St. Thomas Aquinas. Edited by The Aquinas Institute. Green Bay, WI: Aquinas Institute, 2020.

———. *Commentary on the Gospel of John*. Translated by Fabian R. Larcher. Latin/English Edition of the Works of St. Thomas Aquinas, vols. 35–36. Edited by The Aquinas Institute. Green Bay, WI: Aquinas Institute, 2013.

———. *Compendium of Theology*. Translated by Cyril Vollert. Latin/English Edition of the Works of St. Thomas Aquinas, 55:1–237. Edited by The Aquinas Institute. Green Bay, WI: Aquinas Institute, 2018.

———. *Disputed Questions on the Power of God*. Translated by the Dominican Fathers of the English Province. Latin/English Edition of the Works of St. Thomas Aquinas. Edited and Revised by the Aquinas Institute. 2020. https://aquinas.cc/.

―――. *Disputed Questions on the Soul.* Translated by John Patrick Rowan. Latin/ English Edition of the Works of St. Thomas Aquinas. Edited by the Aquinas Institute. 2020. https://aquinas.cc/.

―――. *Faith, Reason, and Theology: Questions I–IV of His Commentary on the* De Trinitate *of Boethius.* Translated by Armand Maurer. Toronto: Pontifical Institute of Mediaeval Studies, 1987.

―――. *The Power of God.* Translated by Richard J. Regan. Oxford: Oxford University Press, 2012.

―――. *Summa contra Gentiles.* Translated by Laurence Shapcote. Latin/English Edition of the Works of St. Thomas Aquinas, vols. 11–12. Edited by The Aquinas Institute. Green Bay, WI: Aquinas Institute, 2018.

―――. *Summa theologiae.* Translated by Laurence Shapcote. Latin/English Edition of the Works of St. Thomas Aquinas, vols. 13–22. Edited by The Aquinas Institute. Green Bay, WI: Aquinas Institute, 2012–2017.

Tillich, Paul. *The Courage to Be.* New Haven, CT: Yale University Press, 1952.

―――. *Systematic Theology.* 3 vols. Chicago: University of Chicago Press, 1951–1963.

―――. *Theology of Culture.* Edited by Robert C. Kimball. Oxford: Oxford University Press, 1959.

―――. "The Two Types of Philosophy of Religion," in *Theology of Culture*, edited by Robert C. Kimball, 10–29. Oxford: Oxford University Press, 1959.

Torrell, Jean-Pierre. *Saint Thomas Aquinas.* Translated by Robert Royal. Vol. 1: *The Person and His Work.* Vol. 2: *Spiritual Master.* Washington, DC: The Catholic University of America Press, 1996–2003.

Weinandy, Thomas G., Daniel A. Keating, and John P. Yocum, eds. *Aquinas on Scripture: An Introduction to His Biblical Commentaries.* New York: T&T Clark, 2005.

Weisheipl, James A. *Friar Thomas D'Aquino: His Life, Thought, and Works.* Garden City, NY: Doubleday, 1974.

―――. "The Principle *Omne quod movetur ab alio movetur* in Medieval Physics." *Isis* 56, no 1 (1965): 26–45.

Wittgenstein, Ludwig. *Tractatus Logico-Philosophicus.* Translated by Charles Kay Ogden. London: Kegan Paul, 1920.

INDEX

kidnapping of Thomas, 5
knowledge of God, 19–20, 63–66, 99–101

Landulf and Theodora (parents of Thomas), 3
Leviathan, 89
Lonergan, Bernard, 104
Lorenzo de Medici, 95
Louis IX, King, 9
love of God, 68–70, 118–120
Luther, Martin, 20, 36, 106
Lyons, Second Council of, 10

magister of theology, 6–7
Malachi, book of, 58
Manichees, 9, 98
manuductiones (leading by the hand), 38
    See also ways (*viae*)
Marx, Karl, 109–110
materialism (ontological), 65
matter, 48–49, 70, 95–96, 99–100
mediator, Jesus as, 30–31
mendicant movement, 4
Merton, Thomas, 42, 83–84, 121
Michelangelo, 95, 98
Middle Ages, 95–96, 113
midlife crises, 10, 117–118
modal transcendence, 56–57
Monte Cassino, abbey of, 3, 5
Moses, 50–51
motion (*motus*)
    argument from, 39–42
    defined, 39, 59, 61
    leitmotif of *Summa theologiae*, 40
Muslims, 8, 20
mysticism
    and Aristotle, 4
    and passivity, 17
    of Thomas, 1–2, 9–10, 92
    See also individual mystics by name

nature-grace interrelationship, 21, 78
necessary beings, 45
Newtonian physics, 19
Nicholas of Cusa, 59–60
nonbeing
    as brought into being, 39, 73, 75
    of evil, 57–58, 85–86
    as threat of finitude, 43, 45–46

noncompetitive relationship between God
    and creatures, 34, 54, 110
    See also God-world relationship
"*Non nisi te, Domine*," 1

Origen, 2, 97–98, 103, 121
otherness of God, 21, 23, 56–57
    See also strangeness of God

pagan philosophy, 20–21, 99
panentheism, 82
pantheism, 54, 72, 82
papal court, 8
passions, 69–70, 99
Paul (Apostle), 24, 63–64
Peter Lombard, 6
Peter of Ireland, 4, 6
philosophy
    Cartesian, 19
    in education of Thomas, 4
    and teaching responsibility of Thomas, 5
    and theology, 20–21, 97
Pieper, Josef, 5, 100–101
Plato and Platonism, 95–100
Plotinus, 92, 99–100
power of God, 48, 58, 73–76, 85
predestination, 31, 105–106
Pseudo-Dionysius, 2, 24–25, 52, 60
puritanism, 99

quaestio disputata (disputed question), 7

Rahner, Karl, 29, 32
rationalism and Thomas, 1–2, 17–18, 39,
    71, 90
Reginald of Piperno, 9–10
Renaissance, 95–96, 113
Resurrection of Jesus, 22–23, 68
revelation, 16–18, 22–24, 28–29, 35, 40, 48
Roccasecca, Italy, 3, 5
Roman Missal, 47
Rudolf Otto, 105

sacra doctrina (sacred doctrine), 16–19, 21–22
    See also theology
sacra pagina (sacred page), 3, 7
sacramental sensibility of Thomas, 100
salus (health), 18